Understanding the Divor

Growing up in a divorced family leads to a variety of difficulties for adult offspring in their own partnerships. One of the best known and most powerful is the divorce cycle, the transmission of divorce from one generation to the next. This book draws on two national social survey data sets to examine how the divorce cycle has transformed family life in contemporary America. Compared to people from intact families, the children of divorce are more likely to marry as teenagers but less likely to wed overall. They are more likely to marry other people from divorced families, more likely to dissolve second and third marriages, and less likely to marry their live-in partners. Yet some of the adverse consequences of parental divorce have abated even as divorce itself has proliferated and become more socially accepted. Taken together, these findings show how parental divorce is a strong force in people's lives and society as a whole.

Nicholas Wolfinger is an assistant professor at the University of Utah. He is the co-editor of the book *Fragile Families and the Marriage Agenda*. He has published widely in journals such as *Demography, Social Forces*, and *Journal of Family Issues*. He is the recipient of the University of Utah's Superior Research Award, 2004.

UNDERSTANDING THE DIVORCE CYCLE

The Children of Divorce in Their Own Marriages

Nicholas H. Wolfinger
University of Utah

CAMBRIDGE
UNIVERSITY PRESS

CAMBRIDGE UNIVERSITY PRESS
Cambridge, New York, Melbourne, Madrid, Cape Town, Singapore, São Paulo

Cambridge University Press
40 West 20th Street, New York, NY 10011-4211, USA

www.cambridge.org
Information on this title: www.cambridge.org/9780521851169

First published 2005

Printed in the United States of America

A catalog record for this publication is available from the British Library.

Library of Congress Cataloging in Publication Data
Wolfinger, Nicholas H., 1966–
Understanding the divorce cycle : the children of divorce in their own marriages /
Nicholas H. Wolfinger.
p. cm.
Includes bibliographical references and index.
ISBN 0-521-85116-5 (hardcover)
1. Adult children of divorced parents – United States – Family relationships.
2. Divorced people – United States – Family relationships.
3. Divorce – United States – Psychological aspects. I. Title.
HQ777.5.W652 2005
306.89 – dc22   2004024988

ISBN-13 978-0-521-85116-9 hardback
ISBN-10 0-521-85116-5 hardback

ISBN-13 978-0-521-61660-7 paperback
ISBN-10 0-521-61660-3 paperback

Contents

Preface

When I started researching the marriage and cohabitation behavior of the adult children of divorce, I was a novitiate in the study of marital breakdown. I grew up in Berkeley, where divorce abounds, but there had been only one divorce in my parents' extensive friendship network. Because the children lived across the street and were my close friends, that one break-up should have affected me, but our skateboarding and family picnicking continued pretty much as before. I was aware that my maternal great-grandmother divorced four times, but my mother always told that story as part of a portrait of Great-Grandma Goodman's exceptional independence, modernity, and colorfulness. (One of her marriages allegedly was to a hereditary nobleman.) I never heard any hint of the trauma my grandmother and great-aunts suffered. My first real exposure to people's thoughts and feelings about marital dissolution came when I mentioned to friends, acquaintances, and strangers on airplanes that I study divorce, and listened to the outpouring of their questions and recollections.

Many people view divorce as unfortunate but sometimes necessary. There are segments of the American population, however, who have intense feelings about it. Some people applaud the availability of divorce, regarding it as a basic freedom, while others deplore it. Each group has its political advocates. In the last fifteen years, more than thirty state legislatures have deliberated legislation that would toughen divorce laws; language urging reconsideration of no-fault divorce appeared in the 2000 Republican Party platform. Even among academics who study divorce, there are some who believe it inflicts little or no harm on children, while others regard it as a source of deep and lasting trauma.

A seminal finding in the scholarly research on families is that divorce seems to be transmissible, and cycles through the generations. First identified in the 1930s, the cycling of divorce has been amply documented by Paul Amato, Larry Bumpass, Norval Glenn, and other distinguished scholars. The crux of the idea is that the family structure of origin powerfully affects marriage formation and marital stability in the adult offspring of divorce. Put simply, the children of divorce are more likely to end their own marriages than are people from intact families. Thus the more children a given divorced couple have, the greater the number of divorces expected in the next generation. With each generation, the number of divorces in that family potentially increases. The astonishing proliferation of divorce in America over the last forty years (with corresponding increases in other Western countries) has become a major social issue.

Many of the findings reported in this book help to flesh out the by-products of the divorce cycle. For example, adult children of divorce (ACDs) are more likely to marry other children of divorce, thereby significantly increasing their probability of divorcing. ACDs are also more likely to avoid marriage altogether. Those who experience multiple disruptions while growing up often dissolve multiple marriages as adults. Lest the reader begin to anticipate that this work is but a lengthy discourse on the perils of divorce, there is a mitigating factor. Early on in my research, I found that since the early 1970s, a growing number of adult children of divorce have succeeded in throwing off the influence of their parents' marital dissolution by creating enduring unions for themselves. (I discuss this slowing of the divorce cycle in Chapter 5.)

Were I to trace here the influence of my great-grandmother's tendency to divorce on successive generations in my family, it would look like an anecdote about the ebb and flow of divorce in twentieth-century America. (My father, a political scientist, is fond of saying that the plural of 'anecdote' is 'data'.) It is my hope that the negative consequences of divorce will continue to abate in the new millennium.

Acknowledgments

This book culminates a decade of research on the long-term consequences of divorce. Throughout these years I enjoyed intellectual and emotional sustenance from many friends and colleagues.

Paul Amato stayed the course, commenting on multiple drafts of the manuscript. Mary Ann Mason was always available for deliberation and support. William Mason, my mentor and dissertation advisor, has been the single greatest influence on my practice of quantitative research. But for the ongoing encouragement and aid of Paul M. Sniderman, this book might have been stillborn.

Lori Kowaleski-Jones, Matthew McKeever, and Andrew Roth deserve special recognition for commenting on manuscript drafts, in addition to providing every conceivable form of professional assistance. My academic career has been enriched by these three friends and colleagues.

For advice and assistance of many kinds at various stages, I thank Sampson Blair, Charles Calhoun, Laura Comay, Glen Elder, Marilyn Elias, Norval Glenn, Fred Greenstein, Diane Hansen, Ruth Klap, Eric Kostello, Sergie Loobkoff, Sasha Loobkoff, Samantha Luks, Steven Martin, David Mechanic, Steven Nock, Christopher Paul, Jerome Rabow, R. Kelly Raley, Nancy Ranney, Judith Seltzer, Ken Smith, Tom Smith, William Sribney, Donald Treiman, Dawn Upchurch, Judith Wallerstein, Carol Kaye, Brad Wilcox, Lawrence Wu, and Cathleen Zick.

At the University of Utah, Brock Fox, Sandra Earl, Trisha Klein Heersink, and Irene Ota provided superlative administrative support; Sonja Anderson, Angela Cassidy, Aldo Hernandez, Ann House,

Andrea McGinn, and Kimberly Shaff furnished expert research assistance. Sonja also did the index, while Aldo made the figures.

Almost at the beginning, the Bireley Foundation backed this enterprise with funding for research assistance, travel, computers, and relief from teaching. I will always remember the Bireleys' confidence in my efforts.

Ed Parsons, my editor at Cambridge, deserves special appreciation for his belief in this book.

This project would not have been possible without two excellent data sets. The National Survey of Families and Households was funded by a grant (HD21009) from the Center for Population Research of the National Institute of Child Health and Human Development. The survey was designed and carried out at the Center for Demography and Ecology at the University of Wisconsin-Madison under the direction of Larry Bumpass and James Sweet. The field work was done by the Institute for Survey Research at Temple University. The General Social Survey was funded largely by a grant (SES-91–22462) from the National Science Foundation. The survey was designed and executed by the National Opinion Research Center at the University of Chicago under the direction of James Davis and Tom Smith.

Special thanks are due to my parents, Raymond and Barbara Kaye Wolfinger, and my wife, Jessica Wolfinger.

ONE

Introduction

> My parents divorced while I was in junior high and it changed my life. I eventually realized it was for the best, seeing in retrospect what a mess they had made of their marriage. I think I learned a lot about what makes a relationship go bad, things that will help me when I decide to get married. One thing is for certain: I will not repeat the mistakes my parents made. The whole thing was really painful, and there is no way I will put myself or my children through it.

I OFTEN HEAR STORIES like that from students in my undergraduate course on divorce and remarriage. These students clearly want to learn from their experiences and do better in their own marriages. But their aspirations face unfavorable odds: Growing up in a divorced family greatly increases the chances of ending one's own marriage – a phenomenon called the divorce cycle, or the intergenerational transmission of divorce.

This book examines how the divorce cycle has transformed family life in contemporary America. Although researchers established years ago that divorce runs in families, many of the details remain unknown. Far too often, divorce transmission is just part of the long and ever-growing list of maladies associated with parental divorce. Not enough is known about the circumstances surrounding divorce transmission, the conditions under which it flourishes, and what decreases the chances that children will repeat the marital experiences of their parents.

Marriage and Divorce: Coexisting American Institutions

Divorce is at least a hypothetical possibility for almost everyone, because almost everybody gets married. Despite well-publicized declines in the marriage rate, at least 90 percent of Americans will wed at some point in their lives.[1] Popular sentiment in recent years has created a very different impression. Past age forty, a *Newsweek* article claimed, American women are more likely to be killed by terrorists than they are to get married.[2] Soaring rates of nonmarital cohabitation have contributed to this impression, as have the well-publicized "fatherless" pregnancies of Madonna, Jodie Foster, and other celebrities. Yet the popular impression is essentially false, the product of minor dips in the marriage rate coupled with substantial increases in the average marriage age. Just as it has been throughout American history, marriage continues to be a normal, expected, and desired way of life for almost all of us.

By the start of the twenty-first century, divorce also had become part of American life. The divorce rate rose throughout much of the twentieth century, really taking off during the 1960s.[3] The divorce boom (as the increases from about 1965–79 have come to be called) remains startling when contrasted with the comparatively low divorce rate of the 1950s. Today, about one in two new marriages will fail. Of children born in the late 1970s, 40 percent experienced the breakup of their families, compared to only about 11 percent of those born in the 1950s.[4] More recently, the pendulum has begun to swing the other way. Since 1979, the divorce rate has stabilized, perhaps in part because people are marrying older and are not rushing into unstable relationships.[5] Nevertheless, the divorce rate remains higher than it was in the early 1960s, before the boom began, and higher than at any other time in American history.

The divorce revolution is much more than a dramatic demographic change. Americans' acceptance (or at least tolerance) of divorce has increased to the point that generally it is no longer construed as a moral failing.[6] Divorced adults and their children do not bear the stigma they once did. Divorced characters are commonplace in today's movies, literature, and television shows.[7] Self-help books covering all aspects of marital dissolution fill our bookstores – a recent trip to my local Borders revealed over fifty titles, and these offerings do not even begin to scratch the surface of the vast academic literature on divorce.

As early as the 1930s, researchers suggested that marital troubles might run in families.[8] More than twenty studies conducted over the last thirty years confirmed that the children of divorce are disproportionately likely to end their own marriages.[9] Additional studies have shown that people from divorced families often avoid marriage altogether.[10] Still other researchers have considered related topics, such as the relationship between parental divorce and marital satisfaction.[11] Despite so many studies, the research literature in this area remains curiously diffuse. There have been no review essays and no monographs devoted to the divorce cycle. Many important questions remain unanswered: Does parental divorce raise or lower offspring marriage rates? To what extent can the timing of marriage explain the relationship between parental divorce and marital instability in their offspring? Does experiencing multiple divorces while growing up increase the likelihood of ending one's own marriage? Do the children of divorce fare worse in second and third marriages? How has the divorce cycle changed over time? What about the effects of parental divorce on cohabitation, a new family form that gained remarkable ground in the last few decades? This book will answer these questions.

Lack of insight into the divorce cycle would be far less significant if divorce itself had only a modest impact on those it touches. Some people do view divorce as a customary (if unpleasant) part of contemporary life.[12] Other people have gone a step further by highlighting divorce's benefits: Unhappy people no longer have to be trapped in loveless marriages; women now enjoy a hitherto unknown economic freedom to seek greener pastures; children fare better if freed from parental conflict.[13] Some writers even seem to welcome divorce, claiming that traditional families offer no significant advantages over single parenting.[14]

Most people dispute neither the right of couples to dissolve a toxic union, nor the benefits of economic conditions that sometimes give women the freedom to leave a bad marriage, nor the contention that it is disastrous for children to be subjected to ongoing parental conflict. That said, it is important to recognize that divorce often does have grievous consequences for both parents and children. Divorced adults report lower levels of well-being, socially and psychologically, than do people who are married, continuously single, or widowed.[15] Divorce often leaves women impoverished – so much so that single mothers are several times as likely as two-parent families to be poor.[16] Economic deprivation while growing up has been linked to poor physical health, diminished intellectual ability and academic achievement, out-of-wedlock pregnancies and births, and various other psychological and social difficulties.[17] Less well known is the fact that divorce shortens the average life span, particularly for men. At age forty-eight, 88 percent of married men will live to age sixty-five, compared to 65 percent of divorced men.[18] For these reasons alone the divorce cycle is worthy of study.

And there is more. Irrespective of its economic consequences, divorce has numerous negative effects on offspring well-being. Compared to people raised in intact families, the children of divorce have more emotional problems, are more likely to drop out of school, and are more likely to smoke, drink, and be sexually active as teenagers.[19] Many of these problems extend into adulthood. People from divorced families on average report worse psychological well-being, more marital problems, and greater alcohol and tobacco consumption than do people from intact families. Perhaps more noteworthy is the fact that adult offspring of divorced families have an approximately one-third greater chance of dying prematurely.[20] Not all children are adversely affected by parental divorce (family structure is only one of many factors responsible for how children fare), but it is strongly correlated with many different aspects of offspring well-being.[21]

Divorce is an important topic for study because it has so many consequences for well-being. Its transmission between generations perpetuates a cycle, adding a whole new dimension. Many families have more than one child; having grown up in divorced families, these children will be more likely to end their own marriages. Thus, each divorce can affect many future marriages.[22] The transmission of divorce between generations, in short, can be thought of as a cascade. Ending a marriage starts a cycle that threatens to affect increasing numbers of people over time, a sobering thought in an era when half of all new marriages fail.

Divorce and Public Policy

California enacted the nation's first modern no-fault divorce law in 1970, making it far easier for state residents to end their marriages. In the next two decades every other state followed suit. Since then, no-fault divorce laws have been attacked repeatedly as the cause of the divorce boom and all its ensuing woes. Make divorce more difficult to obtain (its critics suggest) and numerous social problems can be alleviated. This line of thinking has been partially realized in Louisiana, Arizona, and Arkansas, where "covenant marriage" laws have created two-tiered divorce systems. Couples in these states can now opt for regular marriage (which can be dissolved in accordance with existing no-fault statutes) or covenant marriages (in which divorce is much more difficult to obtain). Grounds for divorce under most covenant marriage laws resemble fault-based statutes of years gone by, and include adultery, abuse, imprisonment, abandonment, or separation for two years.

Despite popular concern about high divorce rates, covenant marriage has so far proved unsuccessful. In Louisiana, for instance, only about 2 percent of couples opt for it. Nevertheless, politicians and family activists continue to push for the modification or repeal of no-fault laws.[23]

The rhetoric of this divorce reform movement often centers on how marital dissolution affects children. Consider the press release that accompanied Rep. Brian Joyce's introduction of antidivorce legislation in the Georgia State House of Representatives:

All around us, every day, we see the bitter fruit of the breakdown of the family. A recent study shows the larger portion of single parent homes are the result of divorce. This contributes heavily to our juvenile crime rate, and accounts for millions of dollars in public assistance to the abandoned families. I believe the breakdown of the family is a direct result of our "no-fault" laws.[24]

This book contributes to current debates on family policy by quantifying the extent to which parental divorce begets offspring divorce, and by identifying the segments of the population for which divorce transmission is most likely.

Outline of Book

In Chapter 2, I try to answer what at first glance might seem an obvious question: Why does parental divorce have such strong effects on offspring well-being in general, and on offspring marital behavior in particular? The answer is far from simple, especially since social-scientific opinion has changed dramatically over time. The initial culprit was thought to be father absence – meaning children need a male role model to develop properly. This notion dominated research prior to the mid-1960s, and to this day remains common. As we will see, it has been discredited. Next, researchers assumed that the consequences of parental family structure had to be attributable to anything *but* divorce or father absence. Economic factors, race- and gender-based discrimination, and stigma were assumed to make all the difference. By the 1980s, social scientists finally started taking a more even-handed approach. Almost no stone was left unturned as researchers used ever-more-sophisticated methodologies to explore almost every aspect of the relationship between parental divorce and offspring well-being. Is it the conflict to which children in divorced families are exposed? Or socioeconomic differences between one- and two-parent families? Maybe it has to do with the neighborhoods in which divorced children are often raised. On the other hand, perhaps children's problems are present long before their parent's marital difficulties ever surface. If this were the case, it might seem that divorce hurt the children, when really it was the children who hurt their parents' marriage. Finally, researchers have even considered whether there may be a genetic component to the divorce cycle. Chapter 2 evaluates all of these explanations, with the intention of identifying the mechanisms that link parental divorce to offspring marital difficulties. Ultimately, I show that the divorce cycle can be attributed primarily to the lessons children learn about relationship skills and marital commitment, and secondarily to the effects of parental divorce on offspring marriage formation and educational attainment. These explanations provide a template for my empirical inquiries into the heritability of divorce.

Chapters 3 through 6 present empirical results. Divorce is always preceded by marriage, so Chapter 3 addresses how the children of divorce go about getting married. Relatively few studies have linked the marital conditions of the children of divorce to their subsequent connubial difficulties. I show that parental divorce affects both marriage timing and the kinds of partners offspring choose. In particular, the children of divorce often marry young and often wed other children of divorce – both choices that bode poorly for marital stability.

In Chapter 4, I show how these and other factors affect the divorce cycle. Children's experiences in nonintact families are varied. Many will have stepparents, and some will see their new families dissolve. I show how these different family types produce different rates of divorce transmission. This chapter also examines whether the divorce cycle persists across various sociodemographic boundaries. Factors that exacerbate or attenuate divorce transmission are identified. Finally, I ascertain whether the children of divorce are likely to dissolve second and third marriages as well as their initial unions. Perhaps people from divorced families enter into ill-fated "starter marriages," then learn from their mistakes and get it right the second time around. The alternative hypothesis is that remarriages have the same problems that plagued participants' initial attempts at matrimony. This is an important issue given that over two-thirds of divorced people remarry.[25]

I then turn to the question of how the divorce cycle has changed over time. Chapter 5 shows that the effect of parental divorce on offspring marital stability has weakened significantly since 1973. To understand this finding, we must consider historical developments in popular attitudes toward divorce. Before the divorce boom, growing up with parental divorce was a much different experience than it is today. The stigma of coming from a "broken home" often interfered with the formation of normal relationships after the divorce, while seeing a parent's marriage fail at a time when divorce was uncommon sent children a stronger message about the impermanence of marital vows than it does today. For these and other reasons, divorce no longer takes such a heavy toll on offspring marital behavior.

Chapter 5 also traces the rapid declines in the marriage rate for the children of divorce. Although all young people are less likely to wed than they used to be, declines in the marriage rate have been especially pronounced for people from divorced families. Turning their backs on marriage, children of divorce have been likely to live with partners out of wedlock in recent years.

Chapter 6 considers how the children of divorce fare in nonmarital live-in relationships. Overall, parental divorce has much weaker effects on the stability of cohabiting relationships than it does on marital stability. I explain this discrepancy by showing that marriage and cohabitation are fundamentally different kinds of relationships. Given the inherent instability of cohabiting unions, incremental disadvantages conferred by parental divorce make little difference. On the other hand, the children of divorce are less likely to marry their live-in partners than are people from intact families.

Chapter 7 summarizes findings with the intention of presenting a comprehensive portrait of the divorce cycle. Although parental divorce can be hard on children, its effects are less severe than they used to be. This finding provides the basis for a discussion of divorce policy. I contend that it would be a grievous mistake for states to weaken or abrogate their no-fault divorce laws. When divorce was rare, parental divorce had much stronger effects on offspring marital behavior than it does today. Returning to the age of tough divorce laws would re-create the social conditions that made divorce harder on children.

Data

Chapters 3–6 are based on analysis of two national data sets: the General Social Survey (GSS); and the National Survey of Families and Households (NSFH). Both provide the advantages typically associated with large national surveys. Sample sizes of over 10,000 people enable study of relatively uncommon phenomena, such as the consequences of experiencing multiple divorces while growing up. National surveys like these also provide a comparison group of people who grew up in intact families. This allows analysts to ascertain what "normal" marital behavior looks like, and how it differs from the behavior of people from divorced families. The NSFH has the advantage of unusually detailed data on marriage and divorce histories, for both respondents and their families of origin. Although not as detailed, the GSS has been repeated annually or biennially over a period of more than thirty years, which makes it possible to show how the divorce cycle has changed over time. Both data sets, along with the methods used to analyze them, are described more fully in Appendix A.

Toward a Balanced Portrait of the Divorce Cycle

This is a fortunate time to be studying marital dissolution. Everyone acknowledges that the divorce rate is high, and it is no longer novel to contend that divorce has lasting consequences for offspring well-being. Substantial improvements in survey data and statistical analysis have made it possible to address new issues, and to address existing questions with far greater precision. Thirty years have passed since social scientists reliably demonstrated that divorce runs in families. The extant research has been useful in identifying the mechanisms responsible for divorce transmission; in other words, the linkage that connects parental divorce to offspring divorce.

The last few years have produced renewed public interest in the consequences of coming from a divorced family. On one side has been the research of Judith Harris, who claims that divorce has absolutely no intrinsic effect on children.[26] Any observable effects, she contends, can be attributed to factors such as genetics and residential mobility. The opposing position is best represented by Judith Wallerstein, whose basic message is that children growing up in a

9

divorced family very often suffer grievous long-term consequences.[27] Prominent among these are erratic patterns of marriage formation and dissolution.

Wallerstein's research has produced a flurry of popular interest, including a cover story in *Time* magazine.[28] For years academic researchers have criticized Wallerstein's work, generally focusing on methodological issues. Instead of a nationally representative sample, her sixty subject families came from seekers of mental health services in affluent Marin County, just north of San Francisco. Many of the parents in these families had preexisting psychiatric problems, and it is no surprise that "troubled parents often raise troubled children."[29] In light of such issues, Wallerstein's findings merit careful scrutiny.

But Wallerstein has brought the consequences of divorce to the fore. Irrespective of the methodological shortcomings, her clinical profiles have been useful in chronicling *what can happen* as a result of parental divorce. What remains to be learned is *how often it happens*. Just how much does parental divorce increase the chances of offspring divorce? How has this relationship changed over time? How does parental divorce affect the union-formation behavior of offspring? What about cohabitation, a new family form that gained remarkable ground in the last few decades? This book will answer these questions.

TWO

Why Divorce Begets Divorce

MOST PEOPLE will be able to provide a ready answer if asked why divorce has negative effects on children: "Kids need fathers" is one likely response. But the absence or presence of a male role model is not what matters most, it seems. Divorce often subjects children to potentially harmful conflict. Moreover, one- and two-parent families have very different economic circumstances, live in different kinds of neighborhoods, and provide children with different home environments. Which of these factors is responsible for the divorce cycle? In this chapter I discuss the theories that have been offered to account for the negative effects of parental divorce on offspring well-being. This will aid in the interpretation of findings presented in subsequent chapters, as well as facilitate an understanding of how divorce research has evolved over time. Ultimately I will show that the divorce cycle primarily can be attributed to the lessons children learn about marital commitment – not to parental conflict or to the absence of male role models. Genetic and demographic differences between people from divorced and intact families play smaller parts in explaining the transmission of divorce between generations.

Two enduring legacies have guided thinking about how divorce affects children. The first involves the intuitive assumption that male role models are indispensable to children's development. The second has much to do with the liberalization of social-scientific thought in the 1960s and 1970s, which led many researchers to blame troubled families on racism and poverty, rather than on the psychological dynamics of divorce. Both ideas have persisted for years, and each has captured the attention of policy makers, social scientists, and the public alike. Although each conception was long held to be incontrovertible, neither can account for the transmission of divorce between generations. Only in the last twenty years have new explanations emerged that better account for the relationship between parental divorce and offspring well-being.

Father Absence

One of the biggest reasons for scholarly and popular interest in father absence is historical: At the beginning of the twentieth century, the proportion of children living in single-parent families was almost as high as it is today. What has changed is the reason for the single parenting. In 1900, before age fifteen approximately one out of four children had a parent die, while about one out of seven children lost a parent to divorce. Combining the two figures suggests that over one-third of children grew up without both biological parents.[1] It was not until the 1940s that divorce finally overtook death as the predominant cause of single-parent families.[2]

Given its history, father absence was the natural place to turn when scholars first tried to account for the effects of divorce on children. For years this explanation dominated the field.[3] A 1978 review of divorce research by Lora Tessman produced conclusions typical of the era: The key to understanding the impact of divorce was how important a male role model is for children's development. When the father was absent, he effectively could be replaced by any male adult assuming an ongoing role in children's lives.[4]

Popular belief also provides a compelling argument for the significance of father absence: Children, especially boys, need male role models; father is the natural choice. This understanding is buttressed by psychoanalytic tenets, given that fathers occupy an important role in Freudian theory. No matter what developmentalists are saying now about Freud and his followers, Freudian ideas pervade the public consciousness: Take away father, and children will have problems. Boys will not learn how to be men; girls will not learn how to relate to men.

I do not question the overall effect of fathers on children's development. But the recent evidence on the role of fathers in accounting for the consequences of divorce has been clear and unambiguous: *Father absence cannot explain the effects of divorce on children.* Almost all early research on the relationship between divorce and children's well-being, therefore, sought proof of a nonexistent relationship.

How do we know that father absence does not matter? The evidence is substantial and wide-ranging. First, and perhaps most important, are consistent findings regarding parental death and stepparenting. Numerous studies have shown that in comparison to divorce, parental death has far fewer adverse consequences for offspring well-being. Of particular interest is the fact that childhood bereavement has no substantial effect on the likelihood that adult offspring will end their own marriages.[5] Both death and divorce deprive children of a male role model. What must really matter, then, are the circumstances surrounding the deprivation. Similar evidence comes from research on stepfamilies. If the children of divorce suffer merely for the lack of a father figure, then children in stepfamilies should fare at least somewhat better than they do in single-parent families. But this is not the case. Children in stepfamilies on average do no better than their counterparts in single-mother families.[6] In some cases, as we shall see, they do far worse: Parental remarriage greatly increases the likelihood that the offspring of divorced families eventually will dissolve their own marriages.

Of course it can be argued that a stepfather is no substitute for the real thing. The work of E. Mavis Hetherington and others shows that family dynamics are often problematic in reconstituted families. Nevertheless, stepfathers engage in many of the parenting behaviors performed by biological fathers.[7] Thus if father absence explained the consequences of divorce, stepfathers should provide *some* benefit to children. But for most outcomes studied by social scientists, including offspring marital behavior, stepfathers do not provide any benefit. If stepfathers do not improve matters, perhaps biological fathers might be in a position to help? Surprisingly, frequent post-disruption contact with biological fathers does not appear to better children's lot.[8]

These findings are only part of the evidence against the notion that father absence is responsible for the effects of divorce on children. Many researchers have operationalized father absence as one of

several competing explanations for the effects of divorce, then evaluated the notion in rigorous empirical tests. Compared with other
explanations (which I will review shortly) the father absence hypothesis fared poorly when accounting for the impact of parental divorce
on offspring educational attainment, premarital child birth, and other
outcomes (the studies did not address the transmission of divorce between generations).[9] Finally, several thorough reviews of the divorce
literature by Paul Amato found no support for the father absence
hypothesis.[10] Despite such a preponderance of evidence, many researchers continue to aver that father absence in itself is a hazard to
children's well-being.[11]

Institutionalized Inequality: Racism, Poverty, and Family Structure

In 1965 the late Daniel Patrick Moynihan, then assistant secretary
of labor and later a prominent senator from New York, authored a
controversial report that brought renewed attention to single-mother
families. The public and scholarly furor that resulted effectively
shaped the agenda for much future research on the implications of
family structure. Almost all problems in the African-American community, Moynihan contended, could be attributed to the proliferation
of single-mother families:

> At the center of the tangle of pathology is the weakness of the
> family structure. Once or twice removed, it will be found to be the
> principal source of most of the aberrant, inadequate, or antisocial
> behavior that did not establish but now serves to perpetuate the
> cycle of poverty and deprivation.[12]

The publication of the Moynihan report in 1965 was a watershed
event in the shift of blame from parents to institutions in scholars'
efforts to explain the deleterious effects of family structure.[13] At the
time, controversies about divorce and single-parenting were nothing
new to Americans.[14] Moynihan's arguments were not novel, nor was
he even describing a particularly new development.[15] Single-parent

families had long been far more prevalent among African-Americans than among whites.[16] Yet Moynihan's report created an indelible impression in the American mind: Single-parenting and the deterioration of African-American communities were inextricably linked. This refocused attention on single-mother families (the overwhelming majority of single-parent families are headed by women) in a way that linked them to race and poverty – topics of interest to policy makers and social scientists alike.

The liberal reaction was swift and intense, perhaps because the Moynihan report appeared retrograde in the context of the Civil Rights movement.[17] Whatever ailed black families had to be anything *but* father absence. Some pointed to lingering racism. Many others cited economic deprivation, eventually coming to base their arguments on well-documented transformations in the American occupational structure.[18] Both lines of thinking shifted the blame from divorce and single-parenting themselves to conditions that genuinely did play a large – although by no means complete – part in explaining the problems associated with mother-only households in the black community. In due time these arguments were extended to all single-mother households.

The ideological revolution was not far behind. In the 1950s there had been stunningly high public approval of what people now call traditional families – married heterosexual couples in which the husband worked and the wife stayed home with the kids.[19] Then the pendulum swung the other way. Single-mother parenting, argued a new wave of feminist thinkers, only looked deviant through the lens of traditionalism. The outcry against single-mother families represented an unreasonable bias in favor of the two-parent archetype supposedly canonized in the 1950s. Newer (or newly conspicuous) family forms – principally single-mother families and unmarried couples living together – all represented viable alternatives to their traditional counterparts.[20] Thanks to a whole collection of *–isms* (sexism, racism, and the like) society had unjustly heaped blame on single-mother families. In time, the feminist position became even more vociferous. Any consideration of pathology within the single-parent family might have a dangerous stigmatizing effect on these very families.[21] So might social policies deliberately targeting single-mother families. Single-mother families, so the feminist argument went, only looked pathological because everyone was treating them as though they were.

When the smoke finally cleared, the feminists and their intellectual allies turned out to be only partially right. There are indeed real and measurable differences between offspring in single-mother families and their more traditional counterparts. Some of these differences, as the work of Sara McLanahan and others have shown, can be explained on the basis of poverty, race, and other demographic culprits.[22] But this is only part of the story. Irrespective of socioeconomic differences, it has become clear in recent years that children from single-parent families do worse in myriad ways. Numerous studies have linked parental divorce to psychological maladjustment, low educational attainment, and an increased predilection for teenage delinquency. Adults from divorced families have worse jobs, make less money, are less happy, have higher divorce rates, and are more likely to be heavy drinkers than their peers from intact families.[23] Certainly not every child of divorce is adversely affected, but in all cases people growing up in nonintact families face higher odds of negative outcomes. In light of these findings, the extreme feminist position regarding the family has become untenable. It can no longer be denied that parental divorce has intrinsic consequences for offspring well-being.

Although the feminist position *in extremis* does not stand up to the evidence, it changed how scholars attempted to account for the consequences of parental divorce. Far more than ever before, social scientists paid attention to how subsequent social and economic circumstances might contribute to the deleterious effects of divorce on offspring well-being. And circumstances do matter: Many of the problems in single-mother families can be attributed to socioeconomic factors, even if others cannot. Conversely, researchers learned that parental divorce can adversely affect anyone, irrespective of social or economic origins.

Toward a Better Explanation

So far I have considered two of the most common explanations for the consequences of parental divorce: institutionalized inequality and father absence. Reflecting a growing awareness of economic and racial inequities, explanations based on institutionalized inequality now seem like an almost inevitable consequence of the 1960s. Father absence dates back much further and has common sense on its side. Only in recent years has dogma taken a backseat to the real reasons divorce affects the marital behavior of adult offspring.

How, then, can we explain the divorce cycle? In the next pages I will review the other explanations that have been proposed to explain the relationship between parental divorce and offspring marital behavior. The story is far more complicated than either of the traditional explanations would lead us to believe. We definitely can point to several factors that we know are responsible, and we can rule out others. Still, we cannot attribute absolute responsibility to any one mechanism.

Predivorce Differences

The first explanation I will consider is perhaps the least obvious: Perhaps it isn't the divorce at all that matters. How could this be? Divorce is almost always a traumatic event for all involved, so how could it not affect children adversely?

Here we must take a step backward and consider the events leading up to divorce. As Diane Vaughan and others have shown, marital dissolution is almost always the culmination of a long sequence of events.[24] Couples who end their marriages may display problems years prior to the breakup. Perhaps these problems, and not the divorce itself, are responsible for how offspring fare. Another possibility is that the kinds of people especially likely to divorce just may not be good parents in certain key respects. They may be, for instance, short-tempered, impatient, irritable, or fickle. So it might not really be divorce that affects children; it might be that certain personality traits or behaviors characterize people who tend to fare poorly in marriage.

A hypothetical example is useful. Susan and Eric have been married about fifteen years. Early on, Eric had occasional bouts of rage: He would yell, smash dishes, and make caustic, hurtful remarks. These incidents were few and far between, and Susan was able to ignore them because Eric had many redeeming features. Then he lost his job. What had been isolated incidents became increasingly frequent, and the marriage deteriorated rapidly. Within a year Susan had moved out, taking twelve-year-old Paula with her. Paula seemed to react badly to the separation. Her grades plummeted; eventually she was arrested for shoplifting.

A researcher might compare Paula with her peers from intact families, then conclude that the divorce was the source of her woes. But as we can see, this might be misleading. Problems in her family, the same sort of problems that ultimately produced the breakup, may long ago have laid the groundwork for Paula's troubles. There is also the possibility here for a reciprocal relationship. Suppose Paula had been a difficult child years before the divorce. This might have put additional strains on Susan and Eric's marriage and expedited their separation. Paula's role in this well may have increased as she grew older. There is evidence that the presence of teenagers in a family increases the likelihood of divorce.[25] Studying this family years later, it might appear that the divorce affected Paula, when really things were more the other way around.

Traditionally, this sort of argument has been hard to test. It requires data on family well-being prior to marital dissolution. This often means tracking families for a number of years, a study design that only recently has become more common. Such surveys are expensive, hence their infrequency. Nevertheless, adequate panel data now exist that allow researchers to ascertain whether preexisting differences between families can explain why divorce hurts children.

The key figure in this research has been Andrew Cherlin.[26] Primarily by following a large British sample, he and his colleagues have shown that predivorce characteristics definitely account for some of the adverse consequences that hitherto had been attributed to divorce itself. Some children in their studies exhibited problems long before their parents actually parted. But predivorce differences cannot by themselves explain all of the relationship between parental divorce and offspring well-being. Regardless of predivorce well-being, parental divorce still has a pronounced negative effect on off-spring marital stability.[27] Divorce represents a dramatic upheaval for children no matter what family life previously had been like.

I will not address directly the possibility of predivorce differences in the current study, because the data sets I use do not permit me to examine family functioning before the breakup. This is a trade-off: My data allow me to draw other conclusions about the divorce cycle (such as the implications of experiencing multiple disruptions while growing up) that would not be possible with most data sets that measure predivorce differences. Furthermore, we know from Cherlin's research that the liability is only partial: His studies show that divorce hurts children irrespective of predivorce differences. Perhaps the most important point to be drawn from these studies is confirmation that divorce is only the culmination of a long series of events. Few marriages end after years of bliss and contentment.

The upshot is more rhetorical than pragmatic. When speaking of how divorce affects children we must acknowledge an entire process, not just the change in demographic and legal status. For almost everybody, parents and children alike, the ultimate consequences of divorce result from an accretion of events.

Context and Community

According to one study, almost 40 percent of women move within a year of marital dissolution. Mobility declines subsequently, but still remains high.[28] Furthermore, frequent moves hurt children irrespective of family structure and social class.[29] Could divorce researchers have been looking in the wrong place? Could it be the mobility, not the divorce, that causes problems for children? It should also be noted that divorced mothers often move to depressed areas.[30] Perhaps these neighborhoods, and not the divorces themselves, take their toll on children.[31]

This argument has been popular recently. Judith Harris contends that parents play a much smaller role in socializing children than previously had been believed.[32] While she also cites genetic arguments, Harris attributes many of the negative consequences of parental divorce to the residential mobility of recently separated mothers.

Harris's argument has some appeal. Without doubt peers are important to children, so it is no surprise that the involuntary disruption of their social lives should take a toll on their well-being.[33] An unwelcome move could only make things worse, given that friends are probably particularly important for children who have recently suffered the trauma of parental separation.[34]

Residential mobility plays a role in explaining the relationship between parental divorce and how children fare, but it is by no means the entire story. Sara McLanahan and Gary Sandefur found that mobility accounts for approximately one-quarter of the relationship between family structure of origin and two outcomes for youth: timely high school graduation for both sexes; and the risk of a teen birth for women.[35]

Although residential mobility has a large impact on the children of divorce, the effect probably does not extend to include adult children's marital behavior. McLanahan and Sandefur's outcomes all concern adolescence and early adulthood. At these younger ages, one's social networks lie close to the parental home and the surrounding school district. These networks may still be in flux, allowing parental divorce to lay the groundwork for teenage pathology. On the other hand, the children of divorce are more likely to be a little older when they come to be in a position to end their own marriages. They will have moved on to new social networks, perhaps centered around college or work, that are not disrupted by their parents' divorce. In short, the physical upheaval of parental divorce is not so recent for this older group.

If residential mobility affects offspring marital behavior, it probably does so in conjunction with the other negative effects of parental divorce. As Judith Wallerstein has noted, divorce disrupts nearly everything familiar about the family.[36] Children experience countless new problems at home. Under these circumstances, their lives outside the home probably assume added importance. Friendships, school social activities, a familiar church, and the like may help cushion the blow of parental divorce. When an unwanted move gets thrown into the mix, things probably get that much worse for children. They lose any remaining stability in their lives. For this reason it is possible that residential mobility exacerbates the negative effects of parental divorce on offspring marital stability. John Hagan and his colleagues offer indirect evidence for this proposition by showing that residential mobility and uninvolved parenting collectively increase the chances that children will fare poorly.[37]

Unfortunately, the data I analyze do not allow me to measure childhood residential mobility. This is one trade-off associated with the National Survey of Families and Households, which I employ because of its detail on respondent family structure throughout childhood. As will be shown in subsequent chapters, changes in family structure are vital in predicting the marital behavior of people from divorced families. Moreover, the established explanations for the divorce cycle (which will be discussed shortly) do not emphasize the importance of residential mobility.

One situation in which mobility affects the children of divorce occurs when a single mother and her children move to a worse neighborhood. This overlaps with socioeconomic explanations for the consequences of divorce, which is my next topic.

Socioeconomic Explanations

By now it is well known that divorce is inextricably linked to economic well-being. Divorce often takes a dramatic toll on women's incomes.[38] Partially as a result, rates of poverty for mother-headed households traditionally have been about five times those for two-parent families.[39] Divorced women's economic plight has shown signs of improvement in the last few years, although they are still doing worse than married women.[40] Furthermore, it is well established that poverty has numerous negative effects on children's well-being.[41] Could divorce affect children only through the financial instability it often induces?

The poverty ensuing from divorce can affect children in at least two different ways. First, life in an impoverished household is inherently less stable. There may be ongoing stress about having enough money to pay for essentials. Single mothers' parenting skills, possibly already debilitated by the trauma of marital disruption, may be further eroded by the struggle to make ends meet.[42] Without a doubt, it is more difficult to grow up in such an environment. Second, parental income may affect the children of divorce through downward geographic mobility: Single-mother families are much more likely to live in depressed areas than are intact families, and poor neighborhoods may offer children fewer social opportunities.[43] Moreover, children in single-mother families are probably overrepresented in less affluent areas. Since the children of divorce are disproportionately likely to participate in deviant activities, their peer groups may contain many troubled youngsters. Could these various privations interfere with children's development, consequently increasing the chances that they will have trouble in their own marriages?

There is now solid evidence that differences in income can explain up to half of the effects of parental divorce on timely high school graduation and premarital fertility.[44] These findings suggest that many of the perceived consequences of family structure actually result from the poverty associated with single-mother households. It is therefore logical to ask whether the divorce cycle also may be an indirect product of poverty. However, the normal sequence of life events makes this seem improbable. Teenage childbirth and failure to graduate from high school both occur during childhood. Most people are at least a few years removed from childhood when they get married and subsequently become divorced. By that time, young adults have distanced themselves from the material circumstances of their families of origin.

Prior studies also suggest that family structure matters more than poverty when predicting offspring marital behavior. Parental income does not affect the likelihood of divorce for people from intact families.[45] People growing up in the Depression, when poverty was commonplace, did not fare poorly in their own marriages.[46] Parental remarriage markedly increases the likelihood that the children of divorce will end their own marriages, and stepfamilies have incomes similar to biological families.[47] Parental education and occupational status do not substantially affect the relationship between parental divorce and offspring divorce.[48] Finally, divorce affects offspring marriage timing irrespective of parental income and education.[49]

Some caveats are in order. First, education and occupational status are not the same things as income. It is conceivable that accounting for income (or changes in income) in the family of origin might attenuate the intergenerational transmission of divorce. This seems unlikely, though: If income were that important, education and occupational status should make some difference. But they do not. Nevertheless, any investigation into the divorce cycle should account for parental socioeconomic well-being, and this will be addressed in the following chapters. Economic well-being does constitute a major demographic difference between single-mother and two-parent families. In addition, socioeconomic status plays such a large role in accounting for other consequences of parental divorce that we should be cautious about disavowing its explanatory power.

Another possibility is that economic well-being in the family of origin might affect the intergenerational transmission of divorce through downward residential mobility. As noted earlier, recently divorced mothers often move into impoverished areas. The children involved may therefore suffer the deleterious effects of poverty from both their families and their neighborhoods. Could neighborhoods have negative effects above and beyond those induced by parental poverty and family structure?

Suet-Ling Pong found that parental divorce, parental income, and school quality all affected eighth-graders' achievement test scores.[50] School quality was measured several ways, including average levels of socioeconomic status among enrolled students and the concentration of children from nonbiological families. The intriguing part of Pong's results, however, was that school quality and parental divorce exerted largely independent effects on children's test scores. Moreover, school quality and family income had independent effects. Pong's findings were confirmed more recently by Carl Bankston and Stephen Caldas.[51]

Results such as these show that divorce takes a toll on children irrespective of neighborhood. It makes sense that academic achievement is an outcome particularly likely to be affected by a social environment full of children from divorced families. Perhaps learning is disrupted in schools where many students experiencing turmoil in their home lives are busy acting out, thereby creating an atmosphere that is not conducive to academic success. It is harder to imagine that chaotic childhood classrooms would produce problems in one's relationships later on, after young adults have distanced themselves from adolescence and moved on to mature lives. The lack of any observed relationship between childhood poverty and adult divorce is evidence that early hardships do not necessarily produce marital difficulties.

Although they probably do not affect children's marital relationships directly, schools may influence the conditions under which people wed, since classmates often marry each other. Since the children of divorce have comparatively low rates of college attendance, a fair number presumably wed partners they met in high school.[52] Furthermore, studies by Frances Goldscheider, William Axinn, and others show that offspring from less affluent families often marry earlier, perhaps because they lack other opportunities.[53] As we will see, marriage timing and mate selection can help to explain the divorce cycle.

Perhaps the most important point to be made about socioeconomic status concerns the relationship between parental family structure and children's academic achievement. It is well established that parental divorce reduces educational attainment, and that low education, in turn, increases the chances of divorce.[54] Prior research has shown that a small portion of the intergenerational transmission of divorce indeed can be explained by low offspring education.[55] Education teaches communication and problem-solving skills that can aid in the resolution of marital difficulties. A college education in particular increases one's capacity for persistence. For these reasons, people with more formal education generally fare better in their marriages; thus education plays a part in the relationship between parental divorce and offspring marital difficulties.

Many of the effects of divorce on children can be attributed to socioeconomic factors. People lacking formal education are more likely to end their marriages, and divorce often leaves families impoverished. Low levels of parental education and income may affect children's life chances, either by fostering a less-than-ideal home environment or by reducing long-term socioeconomic prospects. There is little reason to suspect, though, that low parental education and income ultimately affect the likelihood of divorce transmission. As I will show, the primary reasons for the divorce cycle are linked to family structure *transitions* and not to the economic conditions they engender. Based on prior research, the only socioeconomic component of the divorce cycle appears to be the reduced educational attainment that can result from growing up in a nonintact family.

Genetic Differences

Until recently, the role genetic factors play in the divorce cycle remained unknown. Researchers sometimes speculated that people from divorced families were biologically different from their peers, but these notions were untestable with the sort of survey data generally used to study marital behavior.[56]

These early speculations turned out to be partially correct. Using data from twins, two studies by David Lykken, Matt McGue, and their colleagues have identified a purely genetic basis for the transmission of divorce between generations.[57] Some people, the authors contend, simply have personality traits that are not conducive to maintaining a marriage, and these traits can be transmitted genetically. Children repeat the behaviors of their parents not because of any particular experience they have while growing up, but just because they inherit certain genes.

The genetic explanation can be considered a subset of the "preexisting differences" argument. Divorce again becomes an incidental part of the story. Eric, the husband in our fictional couple, may be prone to bouts of rage for some biological reason. If this were the case, Eric could pass on that suspect gene to his daughter Paula, whose own marriage eventually would be imperiled. In this scenario it does not really matter that Susan and Eric ultimately separated – Paula already had inherited the "divorce gene," and nothing her parents did could change this fact.

This would be a very short book if genetic makeup completely explained marital success. However, the genetic researchers concluded that biology was only part of the story. Many predictors of divorce are purely social in nature. Genetics alone cannot account for why the crude divorce rate increased more than threefold from the 1960s to the 1980s. Biology cannot explain why parental divorce has a much larger effect on offspring marital stability if the breakup occurs while children are under the age of twenty.[58] Genetics also cannot explain why the divorce cycle has weakened over time, one of the findings presented in this book. The divorce cycle may have a genetic component, but genes are far from being the entire story.

Parental Conflict

Parental conflict is perhaps the most important explanation for the effects of parental divorce proposed in the last twenty-five years. It offers a compelling alternative to theories predicated on father absence. It seems obvious: Who does not think it is bad for children to see their parents fight? Indeed, parental conflict can explain many of the negative effects of divorce on offspring well-being. However, conflict cannot account for the divorce cycle. This finding is sufficiently surprising that it warrants explanation.

The conflict argument was first formally articulated in 1982 by Robert Emery.[59] Since then, there has been considerable corroborating evidence. A series of literature reviews by Paul Amato offers overwhelming support for the notion that conflict can explain many of the negative consequences of parental divorce.[60] Various studies find more similarities between children from unhappy but intact families and children from divorced families than between either of these and offspring from happy intact families.[61] Moreover, children from divorced families do worse when parental conflict remains high subsequent to the divorce; post-marital conflict is probably the result of an especially acrimonious divorce.[62] Parental conflict is such a strong predictor of offspring adjustment that children are often better off if their parents choose to dissolve their high-conflict marriages. Under these circumstances, divorce is preferable to continued exposure to quarreling parents.[63]

Applying some of these ideas to their research on the divorce cycle, Paul Amato and Alan Booth found that marital quality in the parental generation strongly predicted several different aspects of offspring marital quality.[64] However, the children of divorce are much more likely to divorce than are people raised by unhappily married parents. Conflict has many negative effects on the marital behavior of offspring, but it is not what makes them end their own marriages. More recent research by Amato and DeBoer clarified this result.[65] Enduring parental conflict often undermines offspring marital happiness, but it simultaneously decreases the chances that divorce will transmit between the generations, because enduring parental conflict teaches children to persevere with their own marriages no matter what happens. This result is extremely useful for understanding the divorce cycle, and I will return to it later.

Role Modeling Redux

I have already ruled out explanations for the divorce cycle based on the absence of fathers as role models, but perhaps role modeling works in other ways. Instead of learning about marital commitment from their parents, the children of divorce may instead learn about marital dissolution. There are several variations on this theme. One of them, the notion that parental divorce reduces offspring marital commitment, turns out to be the most likely explanation for the divorce cycle that has been offered to date.

To understand how marital commitment affects the divorce cycle, it is first useful to rule out other explanations based on role modeling. The first states simply that the children of divorce may be more willing to resort to divorce as a means of dealing with marital difficulties than are their peers from intact families. This line of reasoning implies that the marriages of people from divorced families may not be qualitatively different than other people's. Instead, since their parents have legitimated divorce as a means of dealing with marital difficulties, the children of divorce are simply more inclined to cut their losses should they encounter marital troubles of their own.

It is evidence for this argument that living with a divorced mother often imbues children with less positive attitudes toward marriage and less unfavorable attitudes toward divorce.[66] Nevertheless, this turns out to be a case where attitudes do not accord with behavior. Paul Amato has shown that attitudes toward divorce do not account for the relationship between parental divorce and offspring marital disruption.[67] Asked in the abstract, the children of divorce may see divorce as a good thing. After all, many of them fared better when divorce removed them from acrimonious home lives.[68] It may be an entirely different matter when their own marriages are on the line and when offspring are forced suddenly to apply abstract feelings about divorce in their own lives.

A similar argument states that parental divorce makes single parenting attractive to children.[69] This proposition has three flaws. First, it cannot explain why male children of divorce dissolve their marriages, given that they are as likely as women to succumb to the divorce cycle but rarely gain custody of their own children.[70] If they stand to lose their children, it seems improbable that fathers would dissolve their marriages with the goal of becoming single parents. Second, the appeals of single parenting seem suspect. Many single mothers are poor. Moreover, most divorcées eventually remarry, and many will divorce again. If single parenting were so desirable (the children of divorce might reason), their mothers would not have given marriage a second try. Even if single mothering somehow retains its appeal, the pattern of repeated coupling and uncoupling might not seem overly attractive. Third, the desire to become a single parent cannot explain why the children of divorce dissolve their own childless marriages. Yet today, more than two-thirds of single divorced women do not have children.[71]

A third and final explanation for the divorce cycle based on role modeling concerns marital commitment. Parental divorce reduces offspring commitment to marriage, rather than simply legitimating dissolution as a solution for marital difficulties. As a result, the children of divorce become likely to opt out of troubled marriages. Subtly different from the notion of legitimation, low commitment to marriage is the most convincing argument for the divorce cycle proposed to date.

Almost every marriage has rough spots, but most couples manage to weather the storm. Numerous forces conspire to prevent divorce, including children, social expectations, the legal and religious ramifications of matrimony, financial considerations, and commitment built over time. Perhaps a history of parental divorce changes all that. If relationships seem unstable, they also may seem unsalvageable. The children of divorce may be especially likely to end their own marriages simply because they are ill-equipped to endure the hardships inherent in romantic relationships. Reduced commitment therefore reflects a malfunction that undermines marriage, as opposed to the willful acceptance of divorce as a useful strategy for resolving a troubled relationship. This distinguishes explanations for the divorce cycle based on the intergenerational transmission of reduced commitment from arguments founded on an increased acceptance of marital dissolution.

Compared to some of the arguments cited in this chapter, low commitment to marriage has received little consideration. The most thorough treatment comes from Paul Amato and Danelle DeBoer, who show that people are most likely to divorce when their parents' divorces were preceded by low levels of marital conflict.[72] Children under these circumstances presumably learn lessons about both dealing with interpersonal difficulties and the relative impermanence of marriage: If a marriage runs into trouble, the best solution is to call it quits right away. No other means of resolving the problem may seem tenable. In contrast, offspring experiencing divorce after enduring high levels of parental conflict learn to persist with their own relationships even when difficulties arise.

One manifestation of low commitment might be an exaggerated perception of marital difficulties. The children of divorce often feel that their marriages are in trouble, even though on average their unions are no less happy than the marriages of people who grew up in intact families.[73] A feeling of impending marital doom very well may be the harbinger of a "low commitment" divorce. A study by Norval Glenn and Kathryn Kramer also supports low marital commitment over other explanations for the divorce cycle, on the grounds that rates of divorce transmission appeared to be higher in low-divorce populations than in high-divorce populations.[74] They reason that when children have had less opportunity to observe first-hand how divorce can affect families, parental divorce conveys a stronger message about the fragility of marriage. In contrast, parental divorce in a high-divorce population may not teach children anything about marital commitment that they have not learned already by observing the families around them. Although this evidence for the "low commitment to marriage" theory of divorce transmission is indirect, it accords with the other studies cited here.

Another useful piece of evidence in accounting for the relationship between marital commitment and the divorce cycle is the effect of stepparenting. People whose divorced parents remarry are especially likely to end their own marriages.[75] This finding is consistent with the more general literature on stepparenting, which shows that remarriage does not ameliorate the negative consequences of parental divorce.[76] Although it has not been confirmed that parental remarriage reduces offspring marital commitment, the connection is easily made. By his or her very presence, a stepparent shows that divorce does not signify an irremediable loss; another spouse can always be obtained. In short, the lesson children learn about marriage is easy come, easy go.

Parental Divorce and Offspring Marital Problems

Based on the evidence considered thus far, low marital commitment stands out as the most likely explanation for the divorce cycle. Although this answers the question of why divorce transmission occurs, it falls short of explaining how. Here we must turn to a separate body of literature. Considerable evidence now shows that impaired interpersonal skills play a key role in explaining why people from divorced families have so much trouble in their own marriages.[77] Once

TABLE 2.1. *Some Marital Behaviors Observed in the Children of Divorce*

From Amato (1996: 633–4):
1) Gets angry easily
2) Has feelings that are easily hurt
3) Is jealous
4) Is domineering
5) Is critical
6) Won't talk to the other (spouse)
7) Has had a sexual relationship with someone else
8) Has irritating habits
9) Is not home enough
10) Spends money foolishly

From Webster, Orbuch, and House (1995; Table 4):
1) Shouts when arguing
2) Keeps opinions to self
3) Does not calmly discuss disagreements

From Silvestri (1992: 104):
1) Maladjustment in modesty (too self-critical)
2) Submissiveness (docile, dependent, passive behaviors)
3) Distrustfulness
4) Maladjustment in responsibility (too much or not enough)
5) Inability to self-evaluate
6) Uncooperativeness
7) Hostile passive behavior

Source: Wolfinger (2000), 1064.

marriages strained by problematic interpersonal skills enter a crisis period, low commitment to marriage prevents these couples from resolving their differences.

Paul Amato has conducted the most significant piece of research in this area.[78] He found that the relationship between parental divorce and offspring divorce could largely be explained by a problem behavior scale composed of ten items. These ten items are shown in the first panel of Table 2.1. A study by Webster, Orbuch, and House also identified marital traits common to people from divorced families, though they did not ascertain how these traits contribute to the risk of divorce.[79] These traits appear in the second panel of Table 2.1. A third list of problematic marital behaviors comes from research by

Silvio Silvestri.[80] All three lists reflect significant differences between adult children from intact families and adult children of divorce.

The contents of the three lists vary because each study analyzed a different data set. There are some contradictions: "Domineering" appears on Amato's list, while "submissive" is on Silvestri's. Some of the characteristics listed, especially "has irritating habits," are sufficiently vague as to have little useful meaning. For these reasons, it would be difficult to develop a clinical profile of marital behavior in the children of divorce based on these three lists. Taken together, they make a single basic point: The children of divorce often display behaviors that are inimical to maintaining a relationship. Further evidence for this point comes from three studies that have linked parental marital conflict with offspring marital conflict.[81] By almost any definition, conflict is problematic marital behavior.

At first glance, these findings appear to contradict the fact that the children of divorce do not report lower levels of happiness in their own marriages than do people from intact families. How can marriages strained by conflict or interpersonal difficulties be happy? The answer is that the children of divorce must have a different understanding of marital happiness than do people from intact families: At the very least, offspring from divorced families view marriage less favorably than do people who did not experience parental divorce.[82] Moreover, as noted earlier the children of divorce often feel their marriages are in trouble even when they are happy.[83] All of this suggests that marriage is a much different experience for the children of divorce than it is for people from intact families, a point supported by Stephanie Staal and Judith Wallerstein in their recent qualitative studies.[84]

This understanding sheds light on the relationship between interpersonal difficulties and low marital commitment. Recall that growing up in an acrimonious but intact family increases the likelihood of difficulties in one's own marriage but has little effect on divorce rates.[85] Similarly, parental divorce increases the incidence of problematic behaviors within the marriages of adult offspring, but this in itself may not be sufficient to trigger the divorce cycle. Problematic interpersonal behaviors can certainly strain a relationship, but with sufficient resolve couples may opt to stay married. Add low commitment to the marriage and dissolution becomes much more likely. Parental divorce provides the key ingredient necessary to lower the commitment of offspring, thereby transforming a troubled marriage into a divorce-prone marriage.

From Family of Origin to Marital Dissolution

Let us quickly sum up the explanations for the divorce cycle. First and foremost, parental divorce changes how children feel about marriage. On average, people from divorced families have more marital difficulties than do their cohorts from intact families, and they also exhibit less commitment to staying married. This increases the likelihood that they will end their own marriages.

Less important but nevertheless worthy of mention is the negative effect that growing up in a divorced family can have on the educational attainment of offspring. This may account for a portion of the divorce cycle, given that education is related to divorce risk. Even if the role played by educational differences is trivial, it merits consideration because education is a marker for social status. It is therefore useful to ascertain whether education affects the divorce cycle – both for reasons of intellectual curiosity and for social policy. Given the precedent set by Moynihan's report on African-American family structure, public and scholarly attitudes toward the divorce cycle might be different if divorce only affected the uneducated. For related reasons, it is important to see if race, religion, and other broad social markers affect the transmission of divorce between generations.

A third and final explanation for the divorce cycle concerns the circumstances under which the children of divorce marry. In particular, people from divorced families often marry as teenagers, and youthful marriage is one of the strongest known predictors of divorce.[86] The association between early marriage and subsequent divorce is relatively straightforward. People who marry young may be immature, and may be clinging to adolescent notions about what makes a relationship work. They have not had the time necessary to cultivate the resources – both social and psychological – that successful marriage requires. Furthermore, people who wed at an early age frequently do so despite disapproval from friends and family. If marital difficulties arise, the young spouses may be met with admonitions of "I told you so" rather than the support and advice that might facilitate reconciliation.[87]

The reasons why the children of divorce opt for early marriage are not entirely clear. They will be explored in detail in the next chapter. For now, the important point is that children of divorce sometimes marry under conditions (including their own youthfulness) that ultimately will yield marital problems. Several separate studies have indeed confirmed that the propensity to marry young can explain a portion of the intergenerational transmission of divorce.[88] Marital behavior may facilitate divorce transmission in other ways, and this will be the starting point of my inquiry into the divorce cycle.

THREE

Coupling and Uncoupling

No one can divorce without first getting married. Hence it is important to understand the role marital behavior plays in the divorce cycle. This chapter has two objectives: first, to understand how parental divorce affects marriage timing and rates; and second, to consider the types of people the children of divorce marry. The answers to these questions indicate that the children of divorce often marry under conditions that bode poorly for marital success.

Almost everyone gets married. Despite well-publicized declines in the marriage rate over the past few decades, recent research suggests that the great majority of people – about 90 percent – will wed at some point in their lifetimes.[1] Marriage therefore remains the normal experience for heterosexual Americans, including people from divorced families. Nevertheless, we should not lose sight of the fact that millions of adults will never marry, though many will live with partners out of wedlock – a topic addressed in Chapter 6.

Marriage is often taken for granted, even by social scientists.[2] As a result, we tend to lose sight of its importance. Not only do most people wed, but married men and women on average are happier and better adjusted than either single or divorced people.[3] This is particularly important for the children of divorce, who typically report lower levels of emotional well-being than their peers from intact families.[4] Even though the majority of people from divorced families ultimately will dissolve at least one marriage, a substantial minority will not. For this minority, the benefits of marriage may offset some of the disadvantages associated with coming from a divorced family.

The Demography of Marriage

I begin with a brief look at the demography of marriage. Figure 3.1 presents National Survey of Families and Households (NSFH) data on the timing of first marriages. The rates refer to the probability of wedding at any given age. According to these data, the overall pattern of marriage timing resembles an inverted U.[5] People can and occasionally do marry as early as their first teenage years. Formidable social, legal, and emotional barriers prevent almost everyone from marrying that young, but it is possible, and a tiny minority do so: Approximately 1 pecent of NSFH respondents had married by age fourteen. As people progress through their teenage years, the barriers against marriage gradually fall away, and at some point marriage becomes legal. In all states marriage is not legal until age eighteen, although exceptions are made in certain cases. Parental consent lowers the minimum age to sixteen in many states, while in some states judicial approval or premarital pregnancy can abolish it entirely. The legal marriage age used to be lower in many states. This helps explain why almost 20 percent of NSFH respondents had married by age eighteen. In contrast, only about 5 percent of American teenagers were married as of 2000.[6]

Later in adolescence, the taboos against early marriage recede. Young adults are finishing school, getting jobs, and becoming ready to start families. As a result, marriage rates steadily increase from the teenage years onward. When people enter their twenties (generally considered the prime marriage years), rates gradually reach their apogee. Young adults are now waiting much longer to get married than in previous years: The median marriage age for men is now twenty-seven; for women, it is closer to twenty-five.[7] By that age almost everyone is out of school, employed, and thinking about starting a family as the next step in their lives.

From then on the marriage rate declines. If people have not wed by their late twenties, it becomes increasingly likely that something is keeping them single. Perhaps they have little interest in married life. It is also possible that they simply are not, colloquially speaking, marriage material. Many people still will marry past their late twenties,

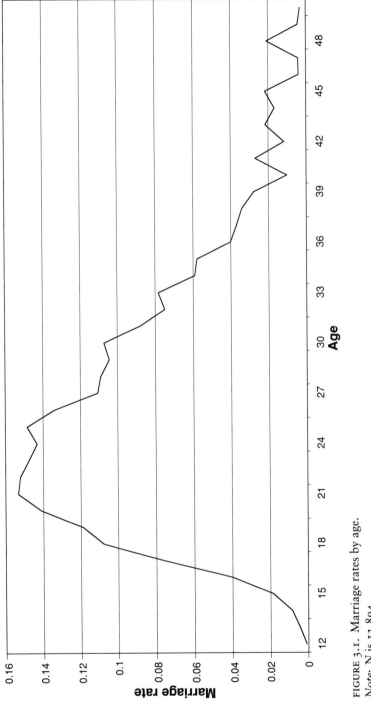

FIGURE 3.1. Marriage rates by age.
Note: N is 12,894.
Source: National Survey of Families and Households, 1987–88.

37

but the rate gradually drops off as prospective spouses are removed from the pool of eligibles. This produces a decline in the marriage rate that continues unabated into middle age and beyond.

The demography of marriage timing provides a framework for understanding how family background might affect overall marriage rates. Early wedlock has the effect of raising the overall marriage rate for any given population, while marriage becomes increasingly unlikely once people enter their thirties. Factors that delay marriage therefore have the ultimate effect of making wedlock less likely. If parental divorce affects marriage timing, the children of divorce will have different overall marriage rates than do people from intact families.

Why Parental Divorce Affects Offspring Marriage Timing

Does parental divorce raise or lower offspring marriage rates? Strong evidence supports both positions. Although more than twenty separate studies have examined the relationship between family of origin and marriage, the results have been strikingly contradictory. Most studies suggest that parental divorce leads to early wedlock, but a sizeable minority find that it tends to delay offspring marriage. Still others find no relationship between family of origin and marriage timing.[8] Furthermore, it is difficult to compare these disparate studies because they employ many different measures of family structure. Some do not distinguish between the varieties of nonintact families, despite considerable evidence showing that parental death has far fewer consequences for offspring marital behavior than does divorce.[9] Other studies only analyze respondents in their early twenties or younger, so comparably little is known about how parental divorce might affect the marital behavior of anyone older.[10]

These issues make it difficult to predict how parental divorce should affect offspring marriage timing and rates. However, previous studies do offer many useful contentions about *why* family might affect offspring marital behavior, and these arguments will be considered next.

The arguments for divorce producing low marriage rates in offspring are simpler, mostly centering on how parental divorce affects the way children feel about romantic relationships. As noted in Chapter 2, parental divorce often leaves children with negative feelings about marriage. This in itself may be enough to discourage matrimony. Recall also that people from divorced families often exhibit behaviors not conducive to maintaining a lasting union. Manifested during courtship, these behaviors may interfere with the formation of intimate relationships.[11] Another explanation for low marriage rates concerns the alternative of cohabitation. Studies by Arland Thornton, Jay Teachman, and others show that the children of divorce often live with their romantic partners out of wedlock.[12] Fearful of repeating their parents' experiences, they may opt for cohabitation as a "safe" alternative to matrimony. This could produce lower marriage rates for people from divorced families. Although marriage often follows cohabitation, living with one partner out of wedlock might delay marriage to someone else. Past a certain age, delaying marriage ultimately makes it less likely to occur.

Three arguments can be offered in favor of the hypothesis that the children of divorce will be inclined to marry young. First, the acrimony preceding, accompanying, and often following a parental divorce frequently creates an unpleasant home environment, and teenagers may marry as a way of getting out. Rates of teenage marriage may be especially high when divorced parents remarry, given that parent-child relations are often strained in stepfamilies.[13] Indeed, studies by Frances Goldscheider, Arland Thornton, and others have found higher rates of marriage for offspring in stepfamilies than in single-parent families.[14] The second explanation for high marriage rates for the children of divorce concerns the grievous consequences divorce has on women's incomes.[15] People from impoverished families often marry at a young age because they lack alternatives, such as the opportunity for a higher education.[16]

The third argument for high marriage rates in the children of divorce is more speculative. Perhaps growing up in a divorced family imbues offspring with an inner loneliness that leads them to seek out romantic involvement. It is evidence for this proposition that the children of divorce often become sexually active at a young age and, if they are women, become pregnant out of wedlock.[17] Parental divorce even accelerates menarche, the onset of menstruation in young women.[18] Matrimony may be an inevitable consequence of premature romantic activity in spite of the fact that parental divorce engenders unfavorable attitudes towards marriage.

Prior research makes it impossible to offer a prediction about whether the children of divorce should be more or less likely to marry than their peers from intact families. Strong arguments support both positions, and this has apparently been reflected in the conflicting findings offered by prior studies. The results presented in the following section should reconcile this inconsistency.

How Parental Divorce Affects Offspring Marriage Timing

I employ data and statistical techniques that permit new insight into the marital behavior of people from divorced families. The data are from the 1973–94 General Social Surveys (GSS) and, in contrast to many previous studies, include adults of all ages. The GSS also includes respondents born throughout the twentieth century, while many earlier studies have analyzed members of only a single birth cohort. Furthermore, I allow the effects of family structure on marriage to vary across the life course, rather than assuming that parental divorce produces uniformly higher or lower rates of marriage at all ages.[19]

The results shown here contrast offspring from single-parent divorced families and stepfamilies with children from intact families. My strategy for presenting results is to report percentages that indicate the higher odds of marriage for offspring from divorced families, compared to offspring of the same age who were raised continuously by both biological parents. Technically speaking, my results represent hazard ratios, computed by exponentiating the metric coefficients produced by event history analyses (or, for select analyses, logistic regression).

As shown in Figure 3.2, prior to age twenty-one both parental divorce by itself and divorce followed by remarriage greatly increase the chances of marriage.[20] At sixteen, for instance, adolescents living with divorced mothers are 123 percent more likely to marry than are

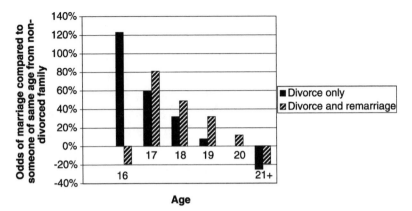

FIGURE 3.2. Parental divorce and offspring marriage timing.
Notes: N is 23,195; 300,464 person-years. Analyses control for race, religion, gender of the primary respondent, presence of siblings, and survey year.
Source: General Social Survey, 1973–94.

people of the same age from intact families.[21] Sixteen-year-old stepchildren are somewhat less likely to marry than are their peers from intact families, but this aberration is probably attributable to the small number of stepchildren who married at sixteen. Otherwise, teenage marriage rates for stepchildren are uniformly higher than for people from other family types, a result consistent with many prior studies.[22] At seventeen, stepparenting increases the likelihood of marriage by 81 percent. At the same age, children in divorced single-parent families have a 60 percent higher marriage rate than do their peers in intact families. For both groups the rates decline steadily, so that by age twenty the children of divorce are only slightly more likely to marry than are people from intact families. From seventeen to twenty, stepchildren have consistently higher marriage rates than do children of the same age in single-parent families.

The pattern of high marriage rates for people from divorced families ends at twenty. After that, their marriage rates dip below those of people from intact families. Stepchildren over age twenty are 19 percent less likely to marry compared to people from intact families; people from single-mother families are 25 percent less likely to marry. There is no appreciable variation for either group after age twenty.

As a result, the children of divorce have lower marriage rates overall than do people from intact families. At the time of the interview, approximately 28 percent of GSS respondents from divorced families had never married, compared to 18 percent from intact families.

Taken together, these results show that the relationship between parental divorce and offspring marriage is complex, involving more than just high or low rates. The children of divorce have high rates of teenage marriage, but if they remain single past age twenty, their ultimate chances of matrimony dip below those of adults from intact families. Failure to account for this life course variation probably explains why prior studies on the relationship between parental divorce and marriage have produced such contradictory results. Historical variation, a second reason for inconsistency in prior studies, will be addressed in Chapter 6.

Demographic differences between respondents cannot explain the marital behavior of people from divorced families. Controlling for race, religion, gender, presence of siblings, rural vs. urban origins, parental education, and respondent education does not affect the relationship between parental divorce and offspring marriage timing. Furthermore, the effects of parental divorce do not vary across these demographic boundaries – everyone is affected the same way.

Why the Children of Divorce Have High Rates of Teenage Marriage

Earlier in this chapter, I presented conflicting arguments predicting both low and high marriage rates for the children of divorce. Since the offspring of divorce experience different marriage rates at different ages, all of the arguments considered earlier may hold true, with one exception.

The children of divorce may be prone to youthful marriage for three reasons, only one of which can be ruled out. Differences in education between divorced and intact families cannot explain why the children of divorce marry young. Unfortunately, the GSS data analyzed here do not measure parental income, which would have permitted a better test of the role parental resources plays in explaining the relationship between family structure and offspring marriage timing. Be that as it may, research by William Axinn and Arland Thornton has shown that parental divorce affects marriage rates irrespective of both parental income and education.[23]

This leaves us with two psychological explanations for high teenage marriage rates in the children of divorce. First, parental divorce produces an early onset of sexual activity that may culminate, perhaps unintentionally, in wedlock. Considerable prior research, cited earlier in this chapter, confirms the propensity for sexual activity in teenagers from divorced families. Unfortunately, the GSS lacks the data necessary to determine if premarital sexual activity or pregnancy contributes to the high teenage marriage rate for the children of divorce. To address this issue, I turn to the NSFH. Although its sample size does not facilitate analyses as detailed as those permitted by the GSS, the NSFH allows identification of marriages preceded by pregnancy. Forty-one percent of respondents from divorced families who wed as teenagers were pregnant or had pregnant spouses. By way of contrast, 32 percent of teenage marriages between people from intact families were preceded by pregnancy. It cannot be assumed that premarital pregnancy always motivated the subsequent marriage, but these figures do support the notion that sexual activity contributes to the high teenage marriage rate of people from divorced families.

Since 59 percent of teenage marriages involving the children of divorce did not involve premarital pregnancy, premature sexual activity cannot in itself account for the patterns of marriage timing described here. Other explanations for high marriage rates must also hold true. In particular, adolescents from divorced families may marry to escape unpleasant home environments. Recall that teenagers reared in stepfamilies have consistently higher marriage rates than do those whose divorced parents remained single. Given the often stressful nature of stepfamily life, stepchildren may have more motivation to take leave of the parental nest than do teenagers in single-parent families. Marriage provides a convenient means of doing so. People raised by stepparents also have higher marriage rates after age twenty than do people whose divorced parents do not remarry. This may occur

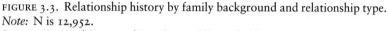

FIGURE 3.3. Relationship history by family background and relationship type.
Note: N is 12,952.
Source: National Survey of Families and Households, 1987–88.

because stepparenting often restores the faith in marriage that children lose subsequent to parental divorce.[24]

Explaining Low Overall Marriage Rates for the Children of Divorce

Past age twenty, marriage rates for the children of divorce dip far below the rates for people from intact families. Earlier in this chapter I proposed two explanations for this finding. First, the children of divorce might cohabit in lieu of marriage. Second, people from divorced families may have difficulty forming lasting romantic relationships.

The GSS lacks adequate information on nonmarital living arrangements, so I use NSFH data to see if people from divorced families cohabit in lieu of marriage. As shown in Figure 3.3, 63 percent of NSFH respondents from divorced families have been married, compared to 81 percent of those from intact families. Combining marriage and cohabitation eliminates a lot of the difference. Seventy-five percent of people from divorced families have been in some sort of live-in relationship – either marriage or cohabitation – compared to 86 percent of people from intact families. The lower marriage rate of people from divorced families therefore partially can be attributed to their proclivity to cohabit. As we will see in Chapter 6, many of these are terminal cohabitations, not leading to marriage.

Cohabitation by itself cannot explain the low marriage rates of people from divorced families past age twenty. After taking both marriage and out-of-wedlock partnerships into account, the children of divorce are still 11 percent more likely than people from intact families never to have been in a live-in relationship of any sort. The same interpersonal difficulties that sometimes deter the children of divorce from marrying also may affect their ability to form cohabiting relationships. Alternately, they simply may choose to eschew marriage as a result of their childhood experiences.

Parental Divorce and Partner Selection: Family Structure Homogamy

Given the amount of prior research on the marriage rates of people from divorced families, curiously little attention has been paid to how they select their spouses. Although early researchers speculated that mate selection might play a role in explaining the divorce cycle, this topic has been explored largely indirectly in recent years.[25] The usual strategy has been to show that certain demographic variables (such as education and age at marriage) can account for a portion of the relationship between parental divorce and offspring divorce. This approach, perhaps popularized by its easy implementation with most data sets, ignores the underlying question: Do the children of divorce choose partners who are poor bets for enduring marriages? The evidence presented so far in this chapter suggests that they do. People from divorced families often marry as teenagers, which in turn greatly increases the chances that ultimately they will get divorced. Furthermore, the children of divorce probably will be overrepresented in poor marriage markets.

Marriage markets refer to the supply and demand of prospective spouses encountered by anyone considering marriage. Since growing up in a divorced family reduces educational attainment and increases the likelihood of teenage marriage, the children of divorce will be

45

overrepresented in marriage markets characterized by both youth and low levels of educational attainment. Thus the children of divorce will be concentrated in marriage markets that contain many fellow children of divorce, and people generally choose spouses from among the people with whom they most often associate. For this and other reasons, the children of divorce may be inclined to marry other people from divorced families. Intermarriage between the children of divorce, which I call *family structure homogamy*, will be the focus of the remainder of this chapter.

Researchers consistently find support for homogamy – marriage based on similarity – on both psychological and demographic bases.[26] Although many people have studied homogamy and many have studied the divorce cycle, no one has examined rates of intermarriage between the children of divorce since Judson Landis did so in 1956.[27] Above and beyond the demographic rationale, there are compelling psychological reasons to expect people from divorced families to choose each other as spouses.

Parental divorce provides a broad common ground of painful and poignant experiences.[28] The instability typical of divorcing families may imbue children with a pervasive lack of trust in their future romantic partners. If they blame themselves for the breakup of their parents' marriages, children of divorce may see themselves as unworthy or incapable of loving, patient, and sustained conjugal relationships. Conversely, children sometimes learn to blame others for interpersonal difficulties. This may be exacerbated by the recriminations often accompanying and following parental divorce. Finally, children may become altogether numb to the exigencies of intimate relationships.

These qualities may become ingrained as the children of divorce grow up, making it hard for them to relate on an intimate level to people who approach the world differently. The children of divorce may even react to people from intact families with anger and jealousy, because they see people brought up in a happy, intact family as having had advantages – emotional, spiritual, and material – that they themselves once had and lost. A prospective mate from a divorced family has had a wealth of similar experiences, and may be able to understand and empathize with the anguish, anxiety, and anger caused by parental divorce, something that people from intact families cannot do.

Similar feelings about marriage also may bring the children of divorce together. As noted earlier, growing up in a divorced family can leave offspring with negative attitudes toward marriage, as well as less unfavorable attitudes toward divorce.[29] Perhaps the children of divorce are inclined to marry each other because they share guarded or pessimistic views of marriage.

Demographic factors may contribute to, or possibly even explain, family structure homogamy. As I have noted, the children of divorce will be concentrated in low education marriage markets, youthful marriage markets, and other markets that face disproportionately high divorce risks. Perhaps these factors can account for the propensity of people from divorced families to marry each other.

How Parental Divorce Affects Partner Selection

NSFH data show that many factors affect the odds of marrying someone from a divorced family. Graduating from college greatly lowers the chances of marrying a child of divorce, a logical result given that people from divorced families are less likely to attend college than are their peers from intact families.[30] Recall that people often meet their future spouses in school. If the children of divorce do not stay in school as long as people from intact families, they face a greater likelihood of meeting and marrying someone without a college degree. Another possibility is that college graduates acquire greater discretion in mate selection, which helps them to avoid potentially high-risk marriages to the children of divorce. This seems improbable, however, because neither parental education nor occupational status appear to affect the chances of marrying someone from a divorced family. Parental socioeconomic characteristics should make at least some difference if education actually increased discretion in choosing a spouse.

Marriage markets probably also can explain why African-Americans are likely to marry people from divorced families. Blacks have higher divorce rates than whites, and most people marry within their own ethnicity. Catholics are less likely to marry people from divorced families, probably on account of their traditionally low divorce rates. Furthermore, the chances of choosing a spouse from a divorced family decline 1 percent per year of age, a result that accords with the findings presented earlier in this chapter. Children of divorce have high teenage marriage rates, but then past age twenty have lower marriage rates than do their peers from intact families, and most people marry within their approximate age group. Furthermore, all of the relationships described so far are net of each other – parental divorce affects offspring marital behavior irrespective of demographic differences between respondents. For example, ethnic differences in education, marriage timing, family structure background, and religion cannot explain why African-Americans are likely to marry people from divorced families.

These results, summarized in Figure 3.4, show that partner selection is an important part of the divorce cycle. The children of divorce often end their own marriages, so it is not surprising that they often marry under conditions, including youthfulness and low levels of education, long known not to be conducive to marital stability. These findings are consistent with a recent study by Jay Teachman, who also finds that the children of divorce frequently form high-risk marriages.[31]

Of greatest interest is the fact that people from divorced families often marry other people from divorced families. Parental divorce raises the odds of marrying a fellow child of divorce by 37 percent. In other words, someone from a divorced family is over one-third more likely to choose a spouse from a divorced family than is a person who did not experience parental divorce. As this figure is net of respondent race, Catholicism, education, marriage cohort, and age at marriage, it does not appear to be an artifact of demographic differences between respondents. Thus the children of divorce appear to marry each other largely for psychological reasons, at least insofar as it is possible to determine with these data.

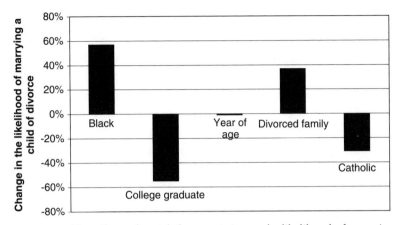

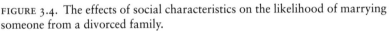

FIGURE 3.4. The effects of social characteristics on the likelihood of marrying someone from a divorced family.
Notes: N is 8,548. Analyses control for marriage cohort, parental education, parental occupational prestige, receiving public aid while growing up, and the other variables shown in this figure.
Source: National Survey of Families and Households, 1987–88.

This evidence for family structure homogamy should be qualified on two counts. First, the NSFH data only measure family structure at the individual level, not the concentration of people from divorced families in any given region. An analysis that accounted for spousal supply as well as demand would provide an optimal test of family structure homogamy. In lieu of data on spousal supply, adjusting results for regional characteristics presumably correlated with divorce rates (including average income, average educational attainment, ethnic diversity, and population density) did not substantially affect estimates of family structure homogamy. Second, demographic differences between respondents can explain a small portion of family structure homogamy. After adjusting for parental socioeconomic well-being, age at marriage, and respondent education, parental divorce increases the odds of marrying someone from a divorced family by 37 percent; without adjusting for differences between respondents, the odds increase by 58 percent. Respondent education accounts for almost all of this difference. Since the children of divorce are less likely to attend college than are people from intact families, fewer children of divorce will be available as prospective mates for people who attend college, so the likelihood of marrying one declines accordingly. In other respects, family structure homogamy affects everyone the same way: Rates do not vary according to respondent religion, ethnicity, age at marriage, or parental socioeconomic background. Perhaps additional control variables not available in the NSFH, such as measures of respondent income or occupational prestige, might further reduce the likelihood that children of divorce marry other children of divorce. Nevertheless, the causes are less important than the consequences, as I will show in the next chapter.

Two more points should be made about family structure homogamy. The first concerns the surprising lack of variation according to family background: Any experience with parental divorce has the same effect on the chances of marrying someone from a divorced family. Remarriage and multiple divorces do not affect the chances of family structure homogamy. This is in marked contrast to nearly all the other phenomena considered in this book. As we saw earlier in this chapter, stepparenting increases the likelihood of youthful marriage. Similarly, Chapter 4 shows that both stepparenting and multiple parental divorces increase the likelihood of ending one's own marriage.

The second point concerns trends in family structure homogamy. As might be expected, the odds of marrying someone from a divorced family have increased over time. Furthermore, these odds have changed at the same rate for people from divorced and intact families. This suggests that the greater likelihood of marrying a child of divorce stems from the fact that marriage markets in recent years simply contain more children of divorce than in years gone by. It does not imply that the psychological mechanisms leading the children of divorce to marry other children of divorce have weakened over time. In contrast to the changes detailed in Chapter 5, this is an unfortunate development. Since marriages between the children of divorce are especially likely to fail, a higher rate of intermarriage among people from divorced families works against other changes that have over time made parental divorce less harmful for children.

Conclusion

The children of divorce often wed under conditions that bode poorly for marital success. Perhaps most important, parental divorce substantially increases the chances of teenage matrimony. Marriage may provide a way out of an unpleasant home environment, or be an unintended result of teenage sexual activity. Either way, the causes are less important than the consequences: Youthful marriage has long been established as one of the most consistent predictors of divorce. As will be seen in Chapters 4 and 5, the propensity to marry young is one of the reasons why the children of divorce have trouble in their own marriages.

Parental divorce also affects offspring marital stability through partner selection. The children of divorce often choose youthful spouses, people with lower levels of education, and other children of divorce. These mate selection patterns – particularly the last one – ultimately increase the chances of marital dissolution.

Family structure homogamy (the propensity for people from divorced families to marry other children of divorce) is interesting in its own right, because it tells us something about how growing up in a divorced family shapes the adult psyche. Divorce somehow affects children in such a way that people who grew up in intact families may seem less attractive as mates. Only fellow children of divorce may understand the pain of a broken home. This is a topic that merits further research attention, optimally through in-depth clinical studies or surveys with detailed psychometric content.

The other noteworthy finding presented here concerns the long-term marriage rates for the children of divorce. Their chances of marriage are high through age twenty, but ultimately decline to approximately 80 percent of the rate for people from intact families. This might be explained by the negative feelings about marriage that parental divorce often instills in offspring. It also makes sense in light of what causes the intergenerational transmission of divorce: If low commitment and impaired relationship skills make it difficult to sustain a marriage, they probably also make it difficult to form long-term relationships.

Many people from divorced families cohabit in lieu of marriage. In Chapter 6, I will show how parental divorce affects these relationships. In the meantime, Chapter 4 will examine how the marital behavior of people from divorced families affects the likelihood of staying married.

FOUR

How Strong Is the Divorce Cycle?

THIS CHAPTER ADDRESSES the prevalence of the divorce cycle. I will answer the following questions:

1) How much does parental divorce increase the chances that offspring will end their own marriages?
2) What demographic characteristics make divorce transmission stronger or weaker?
3) How does the divorce cycle vary by family type, given the diversity of divorced families?
4) Do the effects of parental divorce extend to second and third marriages?

Although some of these questions have been addressed by previous research, another look is warranted for various reasons. The first studies of the divorce cycle are now thirty years old.[1] Statistical techniques have evolved considerably since then, as have data resources. The divorce rate is also higher than it was thirty years ago. The two waves of the National Survey of Families and Households (NSFH), administered between 1987 and 1994, contain extensive detail on respondents' family backgrounds and patterns of relationship formation, yet they have been the basis of almost no research on the divorce cycle.[2]

The advantages of modern statistical techniques and precise data become apparent after taking into account the variety of results produced by prior research. Although all studies confirm that parental divorce increases the likelihood of offspring divorce, there has been little agreement about the strength of the relationship. Another problem has been measures of family structure that lump together various forms of nonintact parenting, making it hard to assess the precise impact of parental divorce on marital stability. In a widely cited article published in 1988, Sara McLanahan and Larry Bumpass showed that white female children experiencing either parental divorce or out-of-wedlock motherhood were 92 percent more likely to end their own marriages than were white women raised by intact families.[3] Considering only parental divorce, Charles Mueller and Hallowell Pope reported a figure of 74 percent for a comparable population.[4] Paul Amato looked at men and women of all races and reported divorce figures of 26 percent (for husbands from divorced families), 59 percent (for wives from divorced families), and 189 percent (when both spouses came from divorced families).[5] Larry Bumpass and his colleagues contrasted people from intact families with all other family types, and obtained divorce figures of 68 percent for husbands, 45 percent for wives, and 49 percent for marriages in which both spouses were from nonintact families.[6] These four studies demonstrate the variability that characterizes prior research.

The results presented in this chapter improve on previous research in several ways. First, I ascertain how the family background of both spouses contributes to marital stability. Few studies have asked this question, and only three have done so using nationally representative data and variables that expressly measure parental divorce rather than simply nonintact parentage.[7] Second, I consider many varieties of divorced families. For instance, no one has considered whether single-parent families, stepfamilies, and twice-divorced families produce different rates of divorce transmission. Third, I analyze relatively recent data from the NSFH using modern statistical techniques. Prior to ten years ago, few studies of the divorce cycle employed event history analysis. Yet this method is crucial for analyzing longitudinal phenomena like marital duration.[8] Taking all of these factors into account will enable me to produce accurate assessments of the divorce cycle under a variety of conditions.

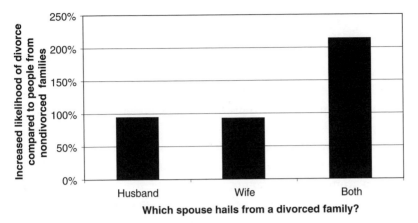

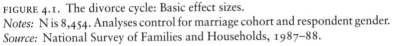

FIGURE 4.1. The divorce cycle: Basic effect sizes.
Notes: N is 8,454. Analyses control for marriage cohort and respondent gender.
Source: National Survey of Families and Households, 1987–88.

How Strong Is the Divorce Cycle?

Do husbands and wives contribute equally to the divorce cycle? How are the chances of marital dissolution affected if both spouses (compared to just one) come from divorced families? Figure 4.1 presents results as the percent increase in the odds of divorce for the children of divorce, compared to people who were not raised in divorced families. Marriages in which either the husband or the wife comes from a divorced family are almost twice as likely to dissolve than are marriages in which neither spouse comes from a divorced family. Marriages between two spouses from divorced families are over three times as likely to dissolve than are marriages between spouses who did not experience parental divorce while growing up. This divorce rate is more than twice as high as the increase associated with just one spouse from a divorced family. In other words, the total risk is greater than the sum of its parts.

Consistent with prior research, my results show that each spouse contributes separately to the chances of divorce. As Paul Amato has pointed out, a marriage containing only one child of divorce may survive if the other spouse brings care and patience to the relationship.[9]

In contrast, the increase in the divorce rate for marriages between two children of divorce is higher than we would expect from the rates associated with individual spouses from divorced families. The potential for discord multiplies in unions where both spouses experienced parental divorce, because (as was suggested in Chapter 2) both partners are more likely to bring low commitment and problematic interpersonal skills to the marriage.

Men and women contribute equally to the divorce cycle, a surprising result for several reasons. Many earlier studies showed that women from divorced families have higher divorce rates than do men.[10] Perhaps the results presented here differ for methodological reasons. Some researchers have analyzed only individual spouses, while others have failed to take into account that, in comparison to women, men are far more likely to misrepresent their own marital histories.[11] Nevertheless, the family backgrounds of wives might be expected to exert a stronger effect on marital stability: Many scholars believe that women contribute more to the emotional upkeep of relationships than do men.[12] Perhaps this emotional upkeep cannot offset the interpersonal difficulties that often characterize marriages involving the children of divorce. This might explain why marriages face the same chances of dissolution whether it is the husband or the wife who comes from a divorced family, but we cannot know for certain.

Although the NSFH contains unrivaled detail on respondents' families of origin, the information on spouses is limited. Accordingly, the remainder of this chapter will focus on the family background of individual partners.

Differences by Family Type

One reason earlier research produced varying estimates of the strength of the divorce cycle is the variety of measures of family structure that have been used. Parental death has minimal consequences for the marital behavior of adult offspring, so combining the children of divorce with the offspring of widows or widowers leads to inaccurate appraisals of the divorce cycle. The children of unwed parents (as I will show later in this chapter) have high divorce rates, but for different reasons than do people from divorced families. To assess the strength of the divorce cycle, it is important to consider how parental divorce alone – and not just nonintact parenting in general – affects offspring marital stability.

Even after taking death and out-of-wedlock birth into account, we must still contend with various family structures. At least two-thirds of divorces are followed by remarriage, and this has consequences for the marital behavior of adult offspring. Second marriages are more likely to fail than are initial unions, so many children will experience a second divorce.[13] If one dissolved marriage can trigger the divorce cycle, it is reasonable to think that a second will exacerbate it. Considerable research has demonstrated that both parental remarriage and multiple divorces make things worse for children, but most of this work has concerned other outcomes besides offspring marital behavior.[14] If multiple transitions (aside from those associated with parental death) adversely affect children, they may well impact offspring marital behavior.

I define a *family structure transition* as divorce or permanent separation, or the addition of a stepparent or a cohabiting partner of a biological parent to any family left incomplete by divorce or separation. This definition is motivated by the understanding (developed in Chapter 2) that the divorce cycle primarily can be attributed to the reduction in marital commitment that children acquire from growing up in a divorced family. Experiencing more than one family structure transition should further emphasize in children's eyes the transitory nature of marriage. In the vast majority of cases, one transition means parental divorce without remarriage, two transitions mean divorce followed by remarriage, and three transitions indicate multiple divorces. The NSFH lacks adequate cases to quantify the effect of experiencing four or more family structure transitions.

Figure 4.2 shows that multiple family structure transitions while growing up greatly increase the chances of ending one's own marriage. Any experience with parental divorce triggers the divorce cycle. The odds of marital dissolution increase with a second transition,

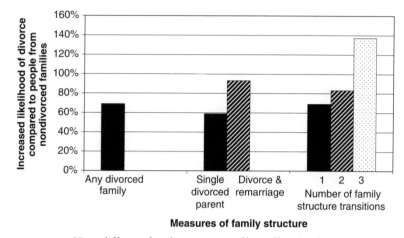

FIGURE 4.2. How different family structures affect offspring divorce risk.
Notes: N is 8,454. Analyses control for marriage cohort and respondent gender.
Source: National Survey of Families and Households, 1987–88.

and are particularly great for people who experienced three or more family structure transitions while growing up. Compared to people from intact families, people growing up with multiple transitions are 141 percent more likely to end their own marriages.[15] By way of contrast, people experiencing one or two transitions face about a 70–80 percent increase. Since one-fifth of young people entering marriage age at the beginning of the twenty-first century will have experienced three transitions, it is significant that multiple transitions have such a large effect on the chances of divorce.[16]

Although any experience with parental divorce increases the likelihood of marital dissolution, multiple transitions clearly make things worse. Numerous studies have therefore oversimplified the divorce cycle. This problem is less important for studies more than twenty years old, because those studies analyzed respondents who grew up in times when far fewer people experienced multiple disruptions. Only 1 percent of NSFH respondents, upon whom these results are based, experienced three or more family structure transitions. Nowadays the numbers are much higher.

This offers a sobering counterbalance to the historical weakening of the divorce cycle that will be explored in Chapter 5. Although the effect of each family structure transition is now weaker, children born in the wake of the divorce boom will experience more transitions. The increased number of family structure transitions young people experience nowadays may work against the declining consequences of any one transition, although it is impossible to know with the data at hand.[17] This might account for a curious finding regarding the changing consequences of parental divorce. In a meta-analysis (a quantitative review) of divorce literature published in 1991, Paul Amato and his colleagues reported that the negative effects of growing up in a divorced family had weakened over time. An updated meta-analysis Amato conducted near the end of the decade, however, showed that the effects of parental divorce once again seem to be growing.[18] Comparing different studies over time is, naturally, a less convincing way of measuring change than is an individual study based on trend data. Meta-analysis always raises the possibility that undetected differences between studies are driving the results. Nevertheless, Amato's finding should lead us to wonder whether the increasing number of family structure transitions children now experience offsets the waning effects of any given transition. This issue awaits future research, with updated data.

Although multiple transitions clearly strengthen the divorce cycle, attention also should be paid to the nature of the transitions. Respondents whose divorced parents remarried have a 95 percent higher chance of ultimately dissolving their own marriages, compared to 60 percent for those whose parents divorced but did not remarry. Unfortunately, it is impossible to know whether the negative effect of parental remarriage has something to do with the character of life within stepfamilies, or whether it reflects the reduced commitment to marriage that results from the ongoing rotation of parental figures. Keeping this in mind, the low commitment explanation is attractive because of its ability to explain the effects of both parental divorce and remarriage. Remarriage likely teaches children that a spouse is replaceable, that another partner can be found if things do not work out with the current one.

Parental Divorce, Social Background, and
Respondent Characteristics

The children of divorce and their families are not statistically average Americans. Divorce rates are higher for certain segments of the population. Parental divorce also has many effects on children beside increasing their odds of marital dissolution. If the social correlates of divorce are not taken into account, the divorce cycle could prove to be nothing more than the by-product of certain respondent characteristics.

Assume that people with blond hair have unusually high divorce rates. Knowing also that hair color is hereditary, we would have to ask whether successive generations of blonds were divorcing because their parents divorced, or just because they inherited light hair, along with its associated risk of marital instability. To address this concern I now turn to the various differences between the children of divorce and people from intact families, then consider how these differences might affect the divorce cycle.

A glance at Table 4.1 shows many contrasts between the children of divorce and people from intact families. Blacks are far more likely than whites to come from divorced families. Catholics are less likely than non-Catholics. These are predictable differences: African-Americans' high divorce rates and Catholic disapproval of divorce are well known. It is more surprising that people from divorced families are 11 percent more likely to be only children. Given that family size does not affect marital stability, it seems likely that divorce gets in the way of additional childbearing. Is it possible that the effects of parental divorce differ if children have siblings?[19] A brother or sister may provide stability against the tumult of a divorcing family. If this were the case, then those children of divorce who come from large families might be less likely to end their own marriages.

There are various socioeconomic differences between intact families and the children of divorce and their families. The data analyzed for this book do not contain a direct measure of income, so two indirect measures – parental occupational prestige and having received public aid – are used as substitutes. Although neither of these is

TABLE 4.1. *Sociodemographic Differences Between People from Intact and Divorced Families*

	Intact Family	Divorced Family
Only child	8%	19%
Has siblings	92	81
Catholic	28%	23%
Not Catholic	72	77
Received public aid while growing up	8%	22%
Did not receive public aid	92	78
Not high school graduate	22%	22%
High school graduate	59	66
College graduate	19	12
Parent(s) not high school graduate	37%	26%
Parent(s) high school graduate	46	54
Parent(s) college graduate	17	20
White	81%	76%
Black	10	16
Other	9	8
Parents' occupational prestige	35 (18)	36 (18)
Age at marriage	22 (5)	21 (5)
Grew up in rural area or small town	65%	51%
Grew up in city or suburbs	35	49

Notes: Underlined numbers are means; numbers in parentheses are standard deviations. NSFH Ns range from 10,484 to 12,946; GSS N is 23,226. All differences between respondents from divorced and intact families are statistically significant except for parental occupational prestige.
Source: National Survey of Families and Households, 1987–88; General Social Survey 1973–94 (data on geographic origins only).

correlated perfectly with income, together they should provide some indication of whether income has any effect on the relationship between parental divorce and offspring marital instability. The other measure of socioeconomic status employed here is education. Educated parents are less likely to get divorced, but if they do they may provide children with cultural and social resources that offset some of the negative effects of parental divorce.[20] For similar reasons, personal educational attainment might also benefit the children of divorce.

Consistent with prior research, Table 4.1 shows that people from divorced families are far less likely to obtain college degrees.

On the other hand, parental divorce has almost no effect on the chances of finishing high school, a surprising result given earlier studies. These findings might be reconciled on the grounds that many studies examine whether parental divorce interferes with *timely* high school graduation. In contrast, I am measuring overall educational attainment.

Also puzzling are some of the results concerning respondents' parents: Non-divorced parents appear to have somewhat lower educational attainment; they are somewhat less likely to have completed high school, if no more likely to have graduated from college. Perhaps divorce motivates single parents – particularly women – to obtain their high school diplomas in order to increase their earning power.

Parental occupational prestige scores do not reveal a big difference, but people from divorced families are three times as likely to have received public aid at some point while growing up. This is not surprising, given the grievous economic consequences of divorce for women. The definition of "public aid" probably also accounts for why that variable shows so much more of a difference between divorced and intact families than do occupational prestige and education. Any history of public aid, even if for a brief interval immediately following a divorce, is measured as receipt. In contrast, education is measured as the highest level reached by respondents' parents, while occupational prestige reflects parental employment at the time respondents were sixteen years old. In many cases, the prestige scores reflect the highest level of parental employment attained when the family was still intact.

Although prior research has not established a link between childhood poverty and marital stability, the difference in the receipt of public aid merits consideration. If only from a policy standpoint, it is important to understand any possible connection between childhood poverty and the divorce cycle. As discussed in Chapter 2, many scholars have alleged that the negative effects of nonintact parenting must be attributable to a greater social ill – like poverty.

Another difference between people from divorced and intact families is average marriage age. Recall from Chapter 3 that the children of divorce have unusually high rates of teenage marriage. This explains why their average marriage age is lower by one year than that of people from intact families. Although the difference may appear small, age at marriage is such a strong predictor of divorce that even one year can be consequential. For instance, a study by Theresa Castro Martin and Larry Bumpass found that people marrying between ages twenty and twenty-two had divorce rates up to 40 percent lower than those who wed as teenagers.[21] The propensity of people from divorced families to marry as teenagers may therefore help explain their high divorce rates.

A final difference between divorced and intact families concerns geographic origins. The NSFH lacks adequate information, so General Social Survey (GSS) data are used to explore the relationship between geographic origins and the divorce cycle. According to Table 4.1, the children of divorce are far more likely to live in urban or suburban areas at age sixteen than are people from intact families. Forty-nine percent of respondents from divorced families grew up in cities or suburbs, compared to 35 percent of people from intact families. Divorce rates are lower in small towns, perhaps because social integration is greater.[22] After divorce, people might be inclined to migrate to cities in search of employment or romantic partners, or perhaps to avoid the stigma of being a single parent in a small town. For these reasons, growing up in a city might have an effect on the divorce cycle. If cities reduce the stigma of ending a marriage, the experience of parental divorce may be different there than in a smaller town or a rural area.

How Social Background and Respondent Characteristics Affect the Divorce Cycle

For purposes of comparison I begin with estimates of the divorce cycle that adjust only for the gender of the respondents and their dates of marriage. These are shown in the first row of Table 4.2. Each subsequent estimate adjusts for all variables considered in previous analyses, in order to determine how each successive variable or group of variables uniquely affects the relationship between parental divorce and offspring divorce.

TABLE 4.2. *The Divorce Cycle: Effects of Adjusting for Sociodemographic Differences Between Respondents*

	Increased Odds of Divorce		
	1 Transition	2 Transitions	3+ Transitions
Base model	69%	83%	137%
Adding controls for race, religion, and siblings	61%	82%	129%
Adding controls for parental SES	54%	75%	117%
Adding control for respondent education	40%	57%	95%
Adding control for age at marriage	40%	57%	78%

Notes: N is 8,454. Analyses control for marriage cohort and respondent gender.
Source: National Survey of Families and Households, 1987–88.

African-Americans have higher divorce rates; Catholics have lower rates. Larger families do not have substantially greater chances of divorce; people from divorced families are disproportionately likely to be only children. Controlling for these differences does not have a substantial effect on the divorce cycle. The second row of figures in Table 4.2 shows that rates of divorce transmission are only slightly lower after adjusting for race, religion, and presence of siblings. Further analyses show that rates of divorce transmission do not vary by any of these characteristics. In other words, parental divorce has the same effect on the marital stability of adult offspring for blacks as for whites, for Catholics as for non-Catholics, and for people from large families or small.

Another difference between people from divorced and intact families concerns the likelihood of growing up in an urban or suburban region, as opposed to a small town or rural area. Even though people growing up in nonurban areas are less likely to end their marriages than are the offspring of city dwellers, this association has no effect on the relationship between parental divorce and offspring divorce. GSS data (not shown in Table 4.2) show that rates of divorce transmission are the same for people raised in big cities and small towns.

Chapter 2 reviewed previous research on the divorce cycle and evaluated factors that might explain the relationship between parental divorce and offspring divorce. Although there is little evidence that parental socioeconomic status (SES) affects the divorce cycle, it is important to rule out the possibility, given the differences in SES between divorced and intact families described earlier in this chapter. On the other hand, Chapter 2 suggested that the effects of parental divorce on offspring educational attainment may account for a portion of the divorce cycle. Furthermore, Chapter 3 established that the children of divorce have high rates of teenage marriage, which in turn may further the divorce cycle. Earlier in this chapter I verified that the children of divorce differ from their peers with respect to both educational attainment and average marriage age. I now ascertain the extent to which all of these factors explain the divorce cycle. In other words, do people from divorced families end their own marriages because of certain sociodemographic correlates of parental divorce, or does parental divorce have an independent effect on the marital stability of adult offspring?

Adjusting for differences in parental occupational prestige, education, and history of receiving public aid slightly attenuates the relationship between parental divorce and offspring divorce, but growing up in a divorced family continues to have a strong impact on offspring marital stability. After controlling for SES, respondents who experienced three family structure transitions face a 117 percent increase in their chances of divorce. This is only 12 percent lower than was obtained without any controls for differences in SES. The attenuation is even weaker for respondents who grew up with one or two transitions, probably because these respondents come from families with higher levels of SES than those experiencing three or more transitions. These results are shown in the third row of Table 4.2.

Parental divorce lowers offspring educational attainment. Furthermore, people with lower levels of education dissolve their own marriages with disproportionate frequency, perhaps because they lack the problem-solving skills that education can encourage. Consistent with prior research, education has a larger effect on the divorce cycle than does any other sociodemographic factor. The effects of three or more family structure transitions again stand out. Adjusting for differences in educational attainment reduces the chances of divorce by 22 percent. The changes in divorce rates for people living through one or two transitions are smaller, but still noteworthy. Nevertheless, parental divorce continues to exert a strong influence on offspring marital stability even after accounting for its adverse effects on educational attainment.

At this point it is useful to reflect back on the order in which I have examined how demographic attributes affect the divorce cycle. I began with traits over which respondents have no control – ethnicity, siblings, parents' socioeconomic characteristics – and then moved on to respondent education. Considering these factors in that order increases confidence in their relationship to the divorce cycle. It is virtually certain, for instance, that the effect of respondent education on marital stability does not have anything to do with unmeasured effects of parental education. Like divorce, educational attainment is transmitted intergenerationally.

The last factor to be considered is the age at which respondents marry. It already has been established that the children of divorce often wed as teenagers. In turn, youthful wedlock is a strong predictor of marital instability. It is not surprising therefore that the relationship between parental divorce and offspring divorce is dampened after adjusting for differences in marriage age. However, only respondents experiencing three or more transitions while growing up are affected; controlling for age at marriage attenuates their rate of divorce transmission by 17 percent. This is a surprising and perhaps anomalous result, given that the GSS data analyzed in Chapter 5 show that youthful marriage affects the divorce cycle for all respondents from divorced families. Earlier studies by Paul Amato, Norval Glenn, and myself also suggest that marriage age helps to explain the relationship between parental divorce and offspring divorce.[23] Since these studies did not identify people experiencing multiple family structure transitions, it is possible that these respondents produced the age-at-marriage effect that had been associated with all children of divorce.

Taken together, all of the demographic differences between people from divorced and intact families can explain at most about one-third of the relationship between parental divorce and offspring divorce. This result best can be conceptualized as the result of a hypothetical experiment: What if the children of divorce were exactly the same as everyone else, except for the family structure changes they experienced while growing up? What if we statistically eliminated other differences between people from divorced and nondivorced families? Would parental divorce still have an adverse effect on offspring marital stability? The answer is yes. Since the divorce cycle is not the product of sociodemographic differences between the children of divorce and other respondents, it must result primarily from the psychological effects of parental divorce. Furthermore, almost all children of divorce are affected the same way. People of all races, religions, and levels of socioeconomic status are susceptible to the divorce cycle.

Can Unwed Motherhood Explain the Divorce Cycle?

The number of children living with mothers who have never married has increased dramatically over time, actually surpassing in 1994 the number of children in single-mother divorced families.[24] This makes it important to understand how nonmarital birth affects offspring marital behavior. Yet this topic has been the focus of almost no research, a stark contrast to the voluminous scholarship on the transmission of divorce between generations.[25]

Out-of-wedlock motherhood has indirect implications for research on the divorce cycle. NSFH data show that children born out of wedlock are far more likely to experience subsequent parental divorce than are children born to two-parent families. Furthermore, out-of-wedlock birth in itself increases the likelihood that adult offspring will end their own marriages. For these reasons it is important to establish that offspring marital instability is really the direct result of parental divorce, rather than out-of-wedlock birth.

Although nonmarital birth adversely affects offspring marital stability, it cannot account for the relationship between parental divorce and offspring divorce. Adjusting estimates of the divorce cycle for the effects of non-marital birth shows that parental divorce still has strong and statistically significant consequences for offspring marital stability. In other words, the connection between out-of-wedlock fertility and subsequent marital difficulties cannot explain the transmission of divorce between generations.

The mechanisms linking out-of-wedlock birth to offspring marital instability must be different from those that trigger the divorce cycle, given that children born to unwed mothers do not learn the same lessons about marital commitment that children experiencing a divorce must absorb. Yet some of the lessons must be similar, as we see from studies on parental cohabitation. Larry Bumpass and Hsien-Hen Lu have shown that about 40 percent of unmarried mothers have cohabiting partners.[26] These relationships often break up, one way or the other: Slightly over 50 percent of cohabitants will wed, and these marriages often end in divorce. (Both premarital childbirth and premarital cohabitation are strong predictors of divorce.)[27] Most cohabiting relationships not ending in marriage will dissolve: Less than 10 percent of cohabitants remain living together out of wedlock after five years.[28]

Given the possibility that parental cohabitation may affect the divorce cycle, both the loss and acquisition of cohabiting partners were counted as family structure transitions as defined earlier in this chapter. Doing so had little effect on the results: The consequences for children's marital stability are similar to when parents' marital relationships only are taken into account. Unfortunately, the NSFH sample does not permit a separate investigation of how the acquisition and loss of partners in cohabiting relationships affects offspring. Even if it did, the results of such an analysis would be misleading. Both cohabitation and out-of-wedlock birth have strong negative effects on offspring well-being.[29] This probably reflects selection effects: It may not be the living arrangements that affect children; it may be that the social and psychological characteristics of people who cohabit and have children prior to marriage are themselves injurious. Without taking these characteristics into account, it would be difficult to understand whether cohabitation dissolution has uniquely negative consequences for offspring marital behavior, or simply reflects the overall negative relationship between cohabitation and child well-being. For all of these reasons, the effects of nonmarital birth on offspring marital stability will not be the subject of further discussion.

A final possibility concerns the effects of parental divorce on the reproductive behavior of female offspring. As noted in Chapter 3, women from divorced families are themselves likely to give birth out of wedlock. Furthermore, unwed mothers who later marry have higher divorce rates than women who give birth while married.[30] Nevertheless, the propensity for out-of-wedlock births cannot explain subsequent marital behavior for women from divorced families. NSFH data show that premarital fertility has almost no effect on the relationship between parental divorce and offspring divorce. In other words, women from divorced families would still have high divorce rates even if they were not prone to having children prior to marriage. Although nonmarital childbirth is a prominent feature of contemporary family demography, it plays little part in the divorce cycle.

Red Herrings

At this juncture it is worthwhile to discuss two factors that have little or no effect on the divorce cycle. They are worth mentioning because traditionally they have been suspected of affecting the relationship between parental divorce and offspring divorce. Recent research suggests otherwise. The two are age at the time of parental divorce, and gender of the custodial parent.

Whenever I lecture on the divorce cycle, my students invariably ask whether the age at which a child experiences parental divorce affects that child's chances for a stable marriage. The reasons for asking are sensible enough. Freud suggested that people are more vulnerable to psychological trauma at particular ages.[31] We are all aware that children move through various developmental stages.[32] Might divorce be particularly harmful at certain times in children's lives? Alternately, do the effects of parental divorce fade over time? This would give younger children the advantage, even if parental divorce affects them the same way it does older children. Although voluminous research has been conducted on these topics, much of it has been inconclusive. Insofar as a clear answer has emerged, younger children seem to fare worse on a variety of outcomes that include eventual marital stability.[33]

Modern developmental theory makes the assumption that children require continued dependence on their parents for optimal growth, so younger children may have trouble achieving appropriate developmental gains subsequent to parental divorce.[34] By the time children become teenagers, they have developed more distinct identities. They are able to separate their needs from those of their parents. This is probably one of the reasons why older children are more likely to react to parental divorce with feelings of relief.[35]

All of these issues are moot in establishing whether older or younger children are more likely to perpetuate the divorce cycle. Divorce timing is important only because it determines children's exposure to remarriage, and subsequently to additional divorces. If a girl experiences divorce as a toddler, it is extremely likely that she still will be living with her mother (or father) if and when remarriage occurs. It is also possible the daughter will be there if her mother's second marriage fails. As I have shown earlier in this chapter, both the remarriage and the second divorce incrementally increase the chances that the daughter will some day end her own marriage. Now consider a son whose parents separate when he is seventeen. By virtue of his age, he probably will move out before his custodial parent remarries. By doing so he avoids first-hand experience with any additional parental relationship transitions and the increased divorce risk they engender. He will fare better in his own marriage, irrespective of any age-specific effects that an initial parental divorce might have had.

A study contrasting these two hypothetical children of divorce probably would find that the daughter was much more likely to have ended her own marriage. A naive researcher might attribute this result to the fact that the daughter had been a toddler when her parents divorced, when the real reason for her own marital difficulties was the additional family structure transitions she experienced by the time she was eighteen and ready to leave the parental household. In short, it makes no sense to consider the timing of the parental divorce because it obscures far more important information.

Another common question concerns the gender of the custodial parent, and whether the effects of parental gender differ for male and female children. The rationale often invoked also concerns differences in psychosocial development, but the answers are different.

Chapter 2 addressed some of the background issues. In particular, I argued that parent absence cannot account for the divorce cycle. Instead, we must look at how the divorce itself affects children. With this in mind, there is no reason why the gender of the custodial parent should have any impact on whether children have trouble in their own marriages. The damage has already been done, a point supported by existing research. An exhaustive comparison across a variety of outcomes, including the intergenerational transmission of divorce, showed no evidence that children's adjustment varies by the gender-pairing of parent and offspring.[36] Furthermore, the NSFH data confirm that male and female offspring fare the same after parental divorce, irrespective of the gender of the custodial parent.

The irrelevance of both gender and divorce timing to the transmission of divorce between generations is not surprising given the results reported in this chapter. The divorce cycle affects almost everybody the same way, irrespective of sociodemographic background. The only really important difference is the number of family structure transitions experienced while growing up.

Multiple Marriages and Multiple Divorces

So far I have focused on first marriages, just as most other scholars of the divorce cycle have. The majority of Americans marry only once, and most data sets only permit study of first marriages. But this does not tell the whole story, because over two-thirds of those who divorce eventually remarry. This raises the question of whether the divorce cycle holds for second and subsequent marriages.

There are two schools of thought here. One is that the factors inherent in parental divorce that produce marital difficulties for

TABLE 4.3. *Predicted Rates of Respondent Divorce, Based on Number of Stressful Transitions in Family of Origin*

Number of Stressful Transitions While Growing Up	Predicted Number of Divorces				
	0	1	2	3+	Total
0	59%	32%	7%	2%	100%
1	50%	36%	10%	4%	100%
2	42%	39%	13%	6%	100%
3+	33%	41%	17%	9%	100%

Notes: N is 8,590. Analyses control for respondent gender, race, religion, presence of siblings, time since first married, missing data on time since first married, and missing data on family structure of origin.
Source: National Survey of Families and Households, 1987–94; Wolfinger (2000), 1075.

offspring their first time around still will be present when the off-spring remarry. Thus, family structure of origin will have the same effect on second marriages that it does on the first. This corresponds to the colloquial notion that some people are divorce-prone, or simply bad bets for lasting romantic relationships.[37] An alternative hypothesis suggests that the children of divorce will fare better in their second marriages than they do in their first (sometimes flippantly referred to as their "starter") marriages, presumably learning from their initial failures.[38] One piece of evidence for this hypothesis is that the children of divorce often marry young, thus starting their initial marriages at an instant disadvantage. They will not be as young the second time around, so they may be more likely to succeed.

Various factors, such as stepchildren, affect the stability of second and subsequent marriages.[39] However, there is no reason to believe that the predictors of remarriage stability differ between people from divorced and intact families. The children of divorce are no more or less likely to bring children into a second marriage.[40] Other characteristics of people from divorced families, such as race and religion, should not affect first and subsequent marriages any differently.

Table 4.3 extends analysis of the divorce cycle to multiple marriages. The results are presented as predicted probabilities, a different format than the other results in this chapter. This makes it easier to compare the effects of various family backgrounds across multiple marriages. Because less than 1 percent of NSFH respondents have divorced more than three times, the table only extends to third marriages.

Parental divorce increases the chances of marital disruption in first, second, and third marriages. Only 2 percent of respondents not experiencing any family structure transitions are likely to end three or more of their own marriages. In contrast, this percentage increases more than fourfold, to 9 percent, for people experiencing three or more transitions while growing up. Conversely, 59 percent of those experiencing no family structure transitions will never end a marriage. For people experiencing three or more transitions, this percentage declines to 33 percent. Overall, the number of predicted personal divorces increases substantially for individuals from unstable families of origin. This is evidence against the notion that the children of divorce have successful relationships once they make it past their starter marriages; parental divorce compromises marital stability in all of their attempts at matrimony.

These findings demonstrate the utility (described earlier in this chapter) of conceptualizing family structure of origin in terms of stressful family structure transitions: People from divorced families often repeat the pattern of unstable relationships they grow up with. The more children experience conjugal relations as transitory, the less commitment they will have to their own relationships later in life.

Conclusion

The divorce cycle is robust. It affects all kinds of people and occurs under a variety of circumstances. Ethnicity, religion, and socioeconomic origins make little difference. This supports the notion that the divorce cycle is directly attributable to the experience of parental divorce, and not to any of the social conditions that often characterize divorcing families.

Parental divorce greatly increases the chances of ending one's own marriage. In this chapter I measured family structure in a variety of ways. Parental divorce increases the chances of offspring divorce by at least 40 percent, irrespective of measures of family structure and adjustments for differences between respondents. When both husband and wife come from divorced families, the odds of divorce are over 200 percent higher. These are sobering figures, especially in light of the fact that the relationship between parental divorce and offspring divorce, as I will show in the next chapter, used to be even stronger than it is now. Nevertheless, the divorce cycle will still present a grievous threat to future generations of newlyweds.

More is worse. Across the board, greater contact with parental divorce increases the chances of ending one's own marriage. Unions in which both spouses come from divorced families have much higher dissolution rates than those containing only one child of divorce. If just one spouse experienced multiple family structure transitions, the odds of divorce also rise.

These results support the explanation for the divorce cycle developed in Chapter 2. Parental divorce reduces marital commitment and interferes with the development of the interpersonal skills necessary to maintain a lasting relationship. This is reflected in several findings. First, unions in which both partners come from divorced families are much more likely to fail than those containing only one child of divorce. With two people from divorced families, the potential for discord multiplies; with only one, the other spouse may exert a stabilizing effect. Second, the children of divorce are as likely to dissolve second and third marriages as they are first ones. This implies ongoing difficulties with romantic relationships, not something resolved after an initial attempt at matrimony. Third, multiple disruptions while growing up incrementally increase the likelihood of dissolving one's own marriages. Every time a child loses a parent, either biological or step, the transitory nature of romantic relationships is further demonstrated. The acquisition of a stepparent only reinforces this lesson. Fourth and finally, controlling for a variety of demographic differences between respondents did not have a substantial effect on the divorce cycle. Although these four findings by themselves cannot confirm the role of marital commitment, they all support it.

74

This chapter has shown that the divorce cycle holds across a variety of conditions. Even the factors that weaken the consequences of growing up in a divorced family, such as education or a later-age marriage, only make small differences. There is, however, one exception to this rule. As divorce has become more common, its transmission between generations has weakened. This dramatic change will be the focus of the next chapter.

FIVE

Historical Developments

THE DIVORCE BOOM is common knowledge. Between the mid-1960s and 1980, rates of marital dissolution skyrocketed from ten divorces per thousand married women to almost twenty-three per thousand by 1979. Less dramatic but still important is the fact that divorce rates rose constantly throughout the twentieth century. The Depression and wars interrupted the overall trend, but the basic story is one of ongoing increase.[1] This is quickly apparent when we consider crude divorce rates over the last eighty years (see Figure 5.1).[2] Only since 1979 have divorce rates stabilized.[3]

In this chapter I consider how the rising level of marital dissolution in the twentieth century has shaped the relationship between parental divorce and offspring marital behavior. The basic story is this: As divorce has become more common, its effects on children have changed dramatically, mostly in a positive direction. In particular, teenage marriage rates have plummeted. Furthermore, the children of divorce now are less likely to get married than are people from intact families, whereas they used to be more likely to marry. The disparity in divorce rates between people from divorced and nondivorced families has considerably narrowed, a development that largely can be attributed to the changing message about marital commitment that parental divorce sends to children. Taken together, these results show that the divorce boom has paradoxically benefitted some of the children caught in its wake.

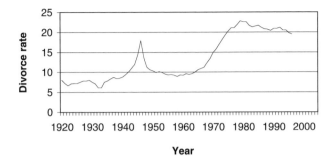

FIGURE 5.1. Annual divorces per 1,000 married women aged 15 and over.
Sources: 1920–67: National Center for Health Statistics, Series 21, no. 24, *100 Years of Marriage and Divorce Statistics* (1973), Table 4; 1968–90: National Center for Health Statistics, Vol. 43, no. 8, *Advance Report of Final Divorce Statistics, 1989 and 1990* (1995), Table 1; 1991–96: United States Bureau of the Census. *Statistical Abstract of the United States: 2000* (120th edition, 2000), Table 144.

How Divorce Changed in the Twentieth Century

Demographers generally speak of divorce in terms of rates, but some simpler facts have worked their way into the public imagination. Approximately one out of two new marriages will end in divorce.[4] Of children born in the late 1970s, 40 percent experienced parental divorce before they reached age eighteen.[5] This figure, of course, is a product of the divorce revolution. Only about 11 percent of children born in the 1950s witnessed the dissolution of their parents' marriages.[6] As is often the case, rates do not tell the whole story. What was divorce like prior to the 1960s? How did people back then view divorcées and their families? How did divorced adults and their children see themselves? Reliable surveys of public attitudes toward divorce only came about at the end of World War II, and even these data have limitations.

In 1945, only 9 percent of the population thought divorce laws in their state were too strict.[7] Attitudes about divorce changed little in the twenty years following World War II, but opinion became much more favorable from the mid-1960s onward. Pro-divorce sentiment apparently peaked in the mid-1970s; in 1974, 34 percent of survey respondents thought it should be easier to obtain a divorce. Since then opinion seems to have cooled, with only 25 percent of the population in 1998 favoring easier access to divorce.

But these figures only tell part of the story. Most surveys only measure whether people think divorce laws should be more lenient, with affirmative answers generally being construed as evidence of tolerant attitudes. This interpretation ignores whether divorce had actually become more readily available. Although attitudes toward divorce laws did not change in the first postwar decades, divorce nevertheless was increasingly easy to obtain. As a result, many survey respondents had no reason to state a preference for more lenient divorce laws. With this in mind, Roderick Phillips was probably correct when he asserted that the public's view of divorce became more favorable throughout the twentieth century, not just since the mid-1960s.[8] It is equally possible that attitudes toward divorce did not grow substantially more pessimistic between 1974 and 1998, as the figures in the previous paragraph suggest; during these years divorce became increasingly accessible to Americans.[9]

Survey data do not capture the experience of divorce in earlier years. Divorce remained heavily stigmatized at least until the 1960s, a point that easily can be substantiated with anecdotal evidence. Some of the stories are startling, especially in light of contemporary views of divorce. They are far more Hester Prynne than *I Love Lucy* or *Leave it to Beaver*.

The force of negative attitudes toward divorce in years gone by– and the extent to which it has waned since then – can be illustrated by considering four twentieth-century presidential candidates, two of whom reached the White House. In 1918, divorce was so morally repellent to Americans that Franklin Roosevelt would have forfeited career, inheritance, and children had he left Eleanor for Lucy Mercer, with whom he had been having an affair.[10] Over thirty years later, Adlai Stevenson's divorce probably contributed to the failure of his presidential campaigns, with voters in 1952 more concerned with his marital problems than with the threat of domestic Communism.[11] One voter told a reporter in 1953, "Young man, the American people proved once and for all last November that we will never tolerate a divorced man in the White House."[12] Twenty-seven years later, Ronald Reagan's divorce was the nonevent of his presidential campaign. In 1996, previously divorced Bob Dole ran for president on a family values platform.

Changing attitudes were reflected in America's changing divorce laws. In 1970, California passed the first modern no-fault divorce law. Other states followed suit over the next twenty years. Although the details varied from state to state, the fundamental principle did not. For the first time, most Americans could obtain a divorce by claiming "irreconcilable differences" or "an irretrievable breakdown" – in other words, by simply asserting that their marriages no longer worked. This represented a significant development from previous years, when one spouse had to sue the other for divorce on serious grounds ranging from adultery to habitual drunkenness to cruelty. The grounds for divorce varied widely from state to state: Some states accepted a variety of reasons, others just one or two. In New York, for example, adultery was the only permissible reason for divorce until 1966. Obviously not all would-be divorcées in that state suffered adulterous marriages, so couples were placed in the embarrassing position of testifying to fictitious sexual escapades in divorce court.

No matter what legal excuses were employed, the consequences of fault-based divorce were similar for the participants. One spouse had to be found legally at fault, often on charges that were deeply humiliating. Imagine, for instance, the courtroom proceedings necessary to establish marital infidelity. Consider the case of Lorimer Linganfield, a Los Angeles resident who successfully sued his wife for divorce on the grounds of adultery in 1920. In court Mr. Linganfield alleged that Mrs. Linganfield had an "appetite for beer and whisky [sic]," that she had a "desire to sing and dance at cafes and restaurants for the entertainment of the public," and that her new bathing suit was "designed especially for the purpose of exhibiting to the public the shape and form of her body."[13] In more recent years, fault-based legal proceedings often became *pro forma*, but a contested divorce could still engender considerable shame and acrimony.

It is hard to imagine that most people divorcing under fault-based statutes would not feel deeply ashamed, and be perceived accordingly. Thus the image of Hester Prynne and her scarlet letter is not far from the truth. Divorce often made pariahs out of children, potentially compromising their affiliations with the institutions – church, classmates, extended family – that might otherwise cushion the blow of a broken home. Nowadays, of course, things are much different. Many people still may frown on divorce, but children are far less likely to lose their friends because their parents' marriage ended.

The conditions under which couples choose to divorce probably also have changed.[14] In the absence of no-fault laws, couples often waited until their marriages had completely deteriorated before seeking a divorce. Normative expectations persuaded quarreling couples to "stick it out" under circumstances such as domestic violence, which today would be readily recognized as reasonable grounds for divorce. When couples finally ended their marriages, the situation may have deteriorated far more than is typical in most divorces today. Less than one-third of modern divorces are preceded by serious conflict, so children experience far less acrimony than probably was typical in the days before no-fault divorce.[15]

No hard evidence supports these assertions. Fifty years ago no one was collecting data on the relationship between divorce and social reputation, or between divorce and conflict. Nevertheless, the consequences of parental divorce are clearly changing. A review of almost 100 studies found that the average negative effect of growing up in a divorced family has declined over time. Parental divorce had far more adverse consequences for offspring self-concept and mother-child relationships in the 1950s and 1960s than in more recent decades.[16] Furthermore, family structure used to have stronger effects on offspring marriage timing than it now does. Mother-only parenting significantly increased the likelihood of early marriage for people born in the 1940s, but not for more recent cohorts.[17] Another study found that parental divorce had fewer negative effects on survey respondents interviewed in 1976 than it did for a comparable sample from 1957.[18] Taken together, these studies provide evidence that the effects of parental divorce have diminished over time. The following pages explore how this trend has affected the marital behavior of adults from divorced families.

Explaining Trends in Marriage Timing for the Children of Divorce

Falling levels of parental conflict may have reduced the teenage marriage rate for people from divorced families. In years gone by, parental conflict probably led teenagers to seek early marriage as a way of escaping an unpleasant home environment. This may have been the case particularly in the 1950s and before, when it was far less common for single people, particularly women, to live on their own.[19] Marriage may have offered the best way out of an unhappy family. Nowadays, if their parents' divorces are less acrimonious than divorce used to be, teenagers will have less incentive to leave.

Marriage rates for the children of divorce may have declined for other reasons. In Chapter 3, I noted that parental divorce may leave children with a sense of loneliness that drives them to seek out romantic relationships. Perhaps this is a reaction to the upheaval children experience in divorcing families. Dating and sexual activity, in turn, may lead the children of divorce to marry as teenagers. If parental divorce involves less acrimony and stigmatization than it used to, then the rate at which the children affected engage in premature romantic activity may be more similar to that of teenagers from intact families. This would drive down the high rate of marriage for teenaged children of divorce.

A final reason for lower marriage rates in the children of divorce concerns the increasing availability of alternatives. As indicated in Chapter 3, the children of divorce have high rates of cohabitation. Furthermore, declines in the marriage rate for the population as a whole largely have been offset by rising levels of cohabitation.[20] Since living with a partner out of wedlock no longer carries the stigma it once did, the children of divorce may have become increasingly likely to cohabit in lieu of marriage. As we will see in the next chapter, parental divorce substantially decreases the chances that a cohabiting union will end in wedlock.

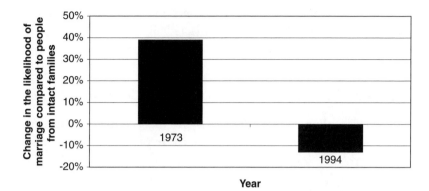

FIGURE 5.2. Trends in marriage timing for the children of divorce.
Notes: N is 23,195; 300,464 person-years. Analyses control for race, religion, primary respondent gender, presence of siblings, duration dependence, and survey year.
Source: General Social Survey, 1973–94.

How Has the Marital Behavior of People from Divorced Families Changed over Time?

To study trends in the marital behavior of people from divorced families, I analyze data from the 1973–94 General Social Surveys. It is no surprise that the overall marriage rate declined during these years, but rates fell especially quickly for respondents experiencing parental divorce.[21] In 1973, people from divorced families had marriage rates 39 percent higher than their counterparts from intact families. By 1994, the children of divorce were 13 percent *less* likely to marry.[22] These results are shown in Figure 5.2.

Chapter 3 established that the effect of parental divorce on marriage timing varies considerably according to age. Teenagers from divorced families have high marriage rates, but past age twenty their chances of matrimony slip below that of people from intact families. Although the chance of marriage has declined for all respondents from divorced families, Table 5.1 reveals considerable age differences. Teenaged children of divorce had high marriage rates in both 1973 and 1994, but the rates went down substantially during these years.

TABLE 5.1. *Increased Marriage Rates for the Children of Divorce by Age and Survey Year*

Respondent Age	1973	1994
Sixteen	152%	72%
Eighteen	86%	27%
Twenty	40%	−4%
Over twenty	4%	−29%

Notes: N is 23,195; 300,464 person-years. Analyses control for race, religion, primary respondent gender, presence of siblings, duration dependence, and survey year.
Source: General Social Survey, 1973–94.

This pattern changes after the children of divorce pass through their teenage years. In 1973, twenty-year-olds from divorced families were about 40 percent more likely to marry than were people of the same age from intact families. By 1994, both groups had almost identical marriage rates, and people over twenty now comprised the great majority of those marrying for the first time.[23] In 1973, children of divorce older than twenty had about the same chances of marriage as did people from intact families, but by 1994 they were 29 percent less likely to marry.

Teenagers from divorced families still have higher marriage rates than their peers from intact families, but the rates are nowhere near as high as they used to be. If the children of divorce have not married by age twenty, they now are disproportionately likely to remain single. Thus for all age groups, the overall trend is a decline in marriage rates. Moreover, this decline cannot be explained by demographic differences between people from divorced and intact families. The falling marriage rate for the children of divorce can be explained neither by socioeconomic well-being for respondents and their families, nor by race, Catholicism, gender, presence of siblings, urban or rural origins.

Why Marriage Rates Have Declined

Earlier I proposed three explanations for the changing relationship between parental divorce and offspring marriage timing; two concern the notion that the typical divorce nowadays involves less conflict and upheaval than it once did. First, if the children of divorce experience less parental conflict, their level of premature romantic involvement no longer may be higher than it is for teenagers from intact families. Fewer romantic involvements might in turn drive down rates of teenage marriage for people from divorced families. Thus if parental divorce is not as harmful to offspring as it once was, the children of divorce now may be achieving more "normal" patterns of marriage formation.

The second explanation also concerns the changing nature of divorce. Divorce and stepparenting can impel teenagers to marry in order to escape unpleasant home environments. Today, if parental divorce has become less unpleasant than it used to be, teenagers will have less reason to leave the nest. It also is much more acceptable now for young adults, particularly women, to move out on their own, so they do not have to resort to marriage in order to escape their families.

These two explanations can account for declining rates of teenage marriage, but they cannot shed light on why young adults in their twenties from divorced families now have lower marriage rates than do their peers from intact families. A weakening of the negative consequences of parental divorce could certainly make teenagers less likely to get married, but levels of marriage for the adult children of divorce should not have dipped below the rate for people from intact families. Put another way, normal marriage rates would be expected from people whose experiences growing up did not affect the development of romantic relationships. The fact that the children of divorce over the age of twenty now are less likely to wed suggests that their experiences growing up are still affecting their relationship formation behavior.

The increased attractiveness of cohabitation as an alternative to marriage could account for low marriage rates for adult children of divorce. In years gone by, people may have wed in spite of negative feelings about marriage: Thirty or more years ago, cohabitation – then rare and frowned upon – may not have seemed like an appealing option. Nowadays, living with a partner out of wedlock is much more socially acceptable. Given that the children of divorce have a strong predilection for cohabitation, they increasingly may be likely to live with their partners in lieu of marriage. Although the available data do not allow me to verify this hypothesis, it seems likely given the facts at hand.

Explaining Trends in the Intergenerational Transmission of Divorce

Marriage timing is not the only consequence of parental divorce that has changed over time. For various reasons, the divorce cycle itself has abated as divorce became more common. Although the explanations are necessarily speculative – no data exist that would allow me to test them – taken together they probably can account for the weakening association between parental divorce and offspring divorce.

Several years ago, when I first started writing about trends in the divorce cycle, I hypothesized that the changing circumstances under which parents choose to end their marriages might be responsible for the weakening rate of divorce transmission.[24] This explanation rested on the notion that parental divorce used to subject children to far more parental conflict than it does now. Offspring would emerge more traumatized and therefore have more trouble in their own marriages.

Since I first formulated this idea, explanations for trends in the divorce cycle based on declining levels of conflict in the parental home have been discredited by the finding that parental conflict decreases the likelihood of divorce transmission, presumably by toughening people's resolve to stick with their own marriages no matter what.[25] Over time, the divorce rate increased, suggesting that people became increasingly inclined to resort to divorce as a solution to their marital difficulties. As divorce became more acceptable, the average level of conflict in divorcing families probably declined, because quarreling couples became less willing to endure ongoing strife. Given that parental conflict decreases the likelihood of divorce transmission,

85

less conflict should have *increased* the rate of divorce transmission, yet the divorce cycle has declined. Thus, alternate explanations must be considered.

Fortunately, there is a viable explanation that accounts for declining rates of divorce transmission while recognizing the role of marital commitment: It concerns the changing message children receive when their parents divorce. Recall that the divorce cycle largely can be attributed to the reduced commitment to marriage that results from growing up in a divorced family. Now apply this understanding historically. The message children received about commitment doubtless was much stronger in the days when almost nobody got divorced. It conveyed a far more poignant lesson if your parents were the only ones in the neighborhood to end their marriage than it does now. Children learned that marriage could be forsaken when it went sour, and that the best solution to marital difficulties might be to cut one's losses. In contrast, no matter how painful it is at the time, a modern divorce does not stand out against the experiences of one's peers, and therefore cannot send nearly as strong a message to children. This is similar to an argument Norval Glenn made to account for demographic differences in the divorce cycle. Divorce transmission is weaker in populations with high divorce rates, he speculated, because marriage itself is seen as less inviolable.[26] If this logic is applied historically, it portends a weakening in the divorce cycle.

Stigma and personal identity are strongly related, as the work of Erving Goffman has shown.[27] It is possible that decreased stigma makes parental divorce less traumatic for children. If they are less likely to see themselves as deviant, and therefore less likely to feel socially isolated, they may be able to have relatively normal childhoods even after their parents' marriages end. As a result, the divorce cycle should be weaker now than it used to be.

Both arguments proposed so far predict that the divorce cycle has weakened because of a decline in the negative consequences of growing up in a divorced family. A third argument concerns the changes in the typical age at marriage for people from divorced families, documented earlier in this chapter. As we saw in Chapter 4, the propensity to marry young accounts for part of the relationship between parental divorce and offspring divorce. The children of divorce may now fare better in their marriages because their rates of teenage marriage have declined. This does not imply a direct weakening of the effects of parental divorce on offspring marital stability. Instead, any historical changes in the divorce cycle depend upon the declining marriage rate for people from divorced families.

How Much Has the Divorce Cycle Abated?

I analyze trends in the divorce cycle using data from the 1973–94 General Social Surveys. The results, summarized in Figure 5.3, are expressed as the increased likelihood of marital dissolution for people from divorced families compared to people who did not grow up in divorced families. Children of divorce interviewed in 1973 whose custodial parents did not remarry were 126 percent more likely to dissolve a marriage than were people who did not experience divorce while growing up. By 1994, parental divorce only increased the chances of divorce by 45 percent, representing a strong decline in the divorce cycle. Growing up in a divorced family still increases the likelihood that adult offspring will end their own marriages, but not nearly as much as in years gone by. In contrast, the rate of divorce transmission did not change over time for people from stepparent families. Between 1973 and 1994 they remained 91 percent more likely to end their own marriages than were people from intact families.[28]

The weakening in the divorce cycle can be attributed in part to the changing marital behavior of people from divorced families. As we have seen, the children of divorce now are less likely to marry as teenagers than they used to be. Moreover, the results presented in Chapter 4 demonstrated that the proclivity for youthful marriage can explain a portion of the relationship between parental divorce and marital stability. This also holds true for the trend in the divorce cycle. After adjusting for age at marriage, parental divorce without remarriage increased the chances of offspring divorce by 94 percent in 1973 and 33 percent in 1994, rates somewhat lower than the

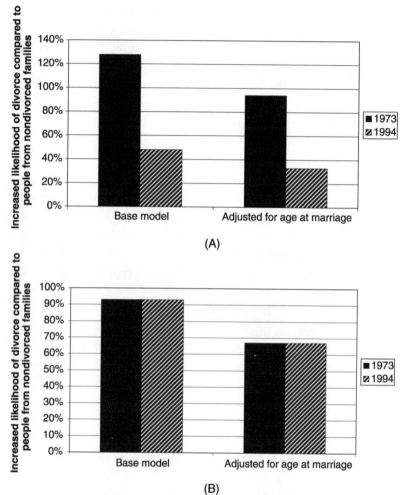

FIGURE 5.3. (A) Trends in the divorce cycle: Parental divorce without remarriage. (B) Trends in the divorce cycle: Parental divorce and remarriage.
Notes: N is 23,357. Analyses control for race, religion, respondent gender, presence of siblings, time since first married, and missing data on time since first married.
Source: General Social Survey, 1973–94.

unadjusted figures of 126 percent and 45 percent. A moderate portion of the decline in the rate of divorce transmission can therefore be explained by the decreasing propensity of people from divorced families to marry young. With lower rates of youthful marriage, the children of divorce now are faring better in their own marriages. However, even after adjusting for changes in marriage timing, a strong decline in the rate of divorce transmission still occurred. This decline confirms that some of the negative consequences of parental divorce have abated as divorce has become more common. Parental divorce no longer appears to hurt children as much as it once did.

Controlling for age at marriage also attenuates the rate of divorce transmission for respondents raised by remarried divorced parents. After adjusting for marriage age, rates of divorce transmission drop from 91 percent to 66 percent for the years of the study. As before, rates for people experiencing both parental divorce and remarriage remained constant between 1973 and 1994.

The stable rate of divorce transmission for people from stepfamilies is consistent with the results presented in Chapter 4. Those results showed that stepparenting strengthens the negative effects of parental divorce on offspring marital stability. Perhaps the adverse consequences of parental remarriage are strong enough to offset the historical changes benefitting people from divorced single-parent families. Another possibility concerns the proposition that declining stigma is responsible for the falling rate of divorce transmission. Stepparent families seem less at risk for stigmatization than do single-parent families. In stepparent families, the semblance (if not the substance) of normalcy has been restored. On the basis of the destigmatization argument for declines in the rate of divorce transmission, there is less reason to expect the lot of stepparent families to have improved in recent years; improvement mostly would be expected for the children of single-parent families. This expectation is borne out by the results, although with the data at hand it is impossible to know for certain why the divorce cycle has weakened only for people whose divorced parents did not remarry.

Demographic differences between people from divorced and intact families cannot explain declines in the divorce cycle. These include socioeconomic well-being for respondents and their families, race, Catholicism, gender, presence of siblings, and whether respondents hailed from urban or rural origins. None of these factors had any significant impact on the changing rate of divorce transmission. Parental divorce affects almost everyone the same way, and this has held true over time.

The declining marriage rate for the children of divorce also raises a less attractive explanation for the weakening divorce cycle. Given that the children of divorce increasingly are likely to avoid marriage altogether, it is possible that those least suited to successful relationships now are those least likely to marry. People from divorced families may be faring better in their own marriages because the pool of married adults no longer contains those left most destabilized by their childhood experiences. This sample-selection hypothesis implies that the negative effects of divorce on children *have not* abated over time.

Falling marriage rates cannot account for the entirety of the decline in the rate of divorce transmission. The rate of divorce transmission fell much more rapidly than did the marriage rate for people from divorced families. Therefore, rates of divorce transmission still would have declined even if marriage rates for people from divorced families had not changed. (A mathematical exposition of this assertion appears in Appendix B.) Perhaps a small portion of the decline in the rate of divorce transmission can be attributed to the fact that the children of divorce now are less likely to get married than ever before. In other words, some of the people who in the past would have gotten divorced now are choosing to remain single or to enter cohabiting relationships. Some of the negative effects of parental divorce indeed have declined, but others have just been obscured by concomitant demographic trends.

It is important to understand that the weakening divorce cycle represents a convergence in divorce rates, not an absolute decline in marital dissolution for the children of divorce. Over the years of the study, divorce rates rose for all respondents for a variety of reasons, most of which are not related to family structure background. But the divorce rate increased more slowly for people from divorced families than for those from intact families, because the negative effects of growing up in a divorced family abated.

Conclusion

Almost everything about divorce has changed dramatically over time. Nowadays people are less likely to remain in troubled or unfulfilling marriages. The stigma of ending a marriage has declined. Today, the children of divorce have the options of cohabiting or remaining single – hitherto discouraged alternatives to wedlock. These developments have had many effects on the marital behavior of people from divorced families.

Marriage rates for the children of divorce declined markedly over time. In 1973 (the beginning of the time series analyzed here), people from divorced families had higher marriage rates than did people from intact families. Rates were especially high for teenaged children of divorce. One reason for this might have been their desire to leave an unhappy home situation. Another might have beeen feelings of loneliness that led to premature sexual involvement.

By 1994, the children of divorce had much lower marriage rates than did people from intact families. Since divorces are not, on average, as rancorous as they used to be, young people probably do not feel compelled so strongly to get married as a way of leaving home. Furthermore, less unpleasant experiences while growing up might have reduced the psychosocial pressures that in earlier years led people from divorced families to marry young. The most likely explanation for declining marriage rates among the children of divorce concerns the increasingly acceptable alternative of cohabitation, a form of relationship that seems particularly appealing to people from divorced families.

Even more dramatic than the declining marriage rate for the children of divorce has been the weakening over time of the divorce cycle. Some of the decline in the intergenerational transmission of divorce can be attributed to the fact that people from divorced families are waiting longer to get married. As a result, the overall marriage pool contains fewer people who are at high risk for marital difficulties.

Most of the declining rate of divorce transmission, however, stems from the fact that parental divorce no longer appears to hurt children as much as it once did. Children do not learn the same lessons about marital commitment that they used to, in part because post-divorce stigma is weaker.

The findings presented in this chapter augur continuing declines in the rate of divorce transmission. As divorce remains common, growing up in a broken home will not send children as strong a message about marital commitment. At the same time, single parents and their children will suffer less stigma. Taken together, these two phenomena make divorce an increasingly normal and common experience. Moreover, today's children of divorce have many fellow sufferers, further emphasizing the normalcy of their shared experience. Children of modern divorces will suffer less on all fronts. If this state of affairs continues, the rate of divorce for adults reared in divorced families may continue to approach divorce rates for those raised by both biological parents. Nevertheless, it seems unlikely that the two rates will ever completely converge. Divorce will always be hard on children, and it will continue to have negative effects.

SIX

The Cohabitation Revolution

IF THIS BOOK HAD BEEN WRITTEN THIRTY YEARS AGO, there would be no need for a chapter on cohabitation. Cohabiting couples were far less common and far more stigmatized – we need only remember the quaint phrase "living in sin" to make that point.[1] Living with a partner out of wedlock used to be something only a few unconventional people did.

No longer. Since the 1970s, rates of cohabitation have risen five-fold. Perhaps even more noteworthy, increases in cohabitation almost perfectly correspond with declines in the marriage rate: Living with a partner out of wedlock is becoming a substitute for marriage for more and more people.[2] As I showed in Chapter 3, this holds particularly true for the children of divorce, whose marriage rates have declined even more quickly than those of the general population. It already has been well established that parental divorce increases the likelihood of entering into a cohabiting relationship.[3] Only three studies have considered how the children of divorce fare in cohabiting relationships, however. Two studies by Kathleen Kiernan and her colleagues analyzed married and cohabiting respondents together, a research strategy that does not permit insight into the unique effects of family structure on offspring cohabitation stability.[4] A third study found no relationship between parental divorce and cohabitation dissolution.[5] No studies have examined whether parental divorce affects the likelihood of marrying one's cohabiting partner. These topics are the focus of the current chapter.

Why are the children of divorce so likely to live with partners out of wedlock? One answer has to do with their feelings about marriage. People from divorced families have less favorable attitudes about marriage and more positive attitudes regarding cohabitation.[6] With the experience of a broken home fresh in their minds, the children of divorce may hesitate to repeat what they perceive to be the mistakes of their parents. So they live with their partners out of wedlock, either to test the waters or to eschew matrimony altogether.

Contrary to the popular stereotype of carefree college students, cohabitation is most common among people who have not attended college.[7] Although parental divorce reduces offspring educational attainment, this relationship cannot account for why people from divorced families often live with partners out of wedlock: If all young adults had identical socioeconomic backgrounds, those from divorced families would still have higher rates of cohabitation.[8]

A second reason for high cohabitation rates among the children of divorce is directly related to the divorce cycle. Divorced adults have higher rates of cohabitation than people who have never been married.[9] Having given marriage a try, many people are loath to risk a second failure. Cohabitation may seem like a safe alternative. Since the children of divorce are so likely to end their own marriages, many will cohabit in lieu of remarriage. If we add these people to those who reject marriage in the first place, we have a large and growing population of cohabitors. Therein lies the necessity for a chapter on cohabitation: Focusing only on marriage would overlook the experiences of a sizeable contingent of people from divorced families.

In a broader sense, cohabitation would be relevant to the divorce cycle even if people from divorced families were not so likely to live with partners out of wedlock. Parental divorce and cohabitation are both symbolic of the modern family, evidence of its decline in the eyes of many. Both became prevalent and conspicuous around the same time, in the latter third of the twentieth century. If a book on the divorce cycle is viewed as a primer on newer family forms, it could hardly avoid a section on cohabitation.

How Marriage and Cohabitation Differ

It is useful at this juncture to take a brief look at the nature of cohabiting relationships. Although scholars know far less about cohabitation

than about marriage, the last ten or so years have seen enough research to establish that the two are indeed very different. These differences, as we soon shall see, have many implications for the divorce
cycle.

People today bemoan the high divorce rate, but marriage is the
apotheosis of stability compared to cohabitation. Five years after
moving in, less than one in ten couples still live together out of wedlock. Slightly over half of cohabiting couples get married, and most
will do so within a few years after moving in together.[10] The typical
course of a cohabiting relationship is also different. This is apparent
from Figure 6.1, which shows the rates of departure from a cohabiting relationship at any given point. Generally there are two ways to
exit a cohabiting union: marriage or dissolution. Of course a partner may die, but usually this has no reflection on the quality of the
relationship, and in any event most cohabitors are relatively young.[11]

Although most cohabitors eventually will wed, the longer they live
together the less likely they are to get married. Given that the majority plan to marry, many probably move in together just prior to
the wedding.[12] But the more interesting story concerns the chances
of dissolution, which remain fairly constant throughout the five-year
interval shown in Figure 6.1. This represents a striking difference
from marriage. Married couples face a high rate of divorce during
the first few years of wedlock, presumably during the time they establish compatibility. After that, divorce rates steadily go down.[13] Time
together builds commitment and weeds out unsuccessful unions. In
contrast, the constant dissolution rate for cohabitation implies a relationship with little commitment. Irrespective of how long the two
have lived together, any cohabiting couple is equally likely to break
up at any time. More than any study of relationship quality, this finding speaks volumes about the nature of the cohabitating partnership:
It is a fundamentally uncommitted union, and prone to spontaneous
dissolution.[14]

Although parental divorce has a strong effect on marital stability,
it is difficult to predict exactly how the children of divorce will fare in
their cohabiting relationships. Because cohabiting unions are on the
whole fundamentally unstable, it may take little to break them up.

95

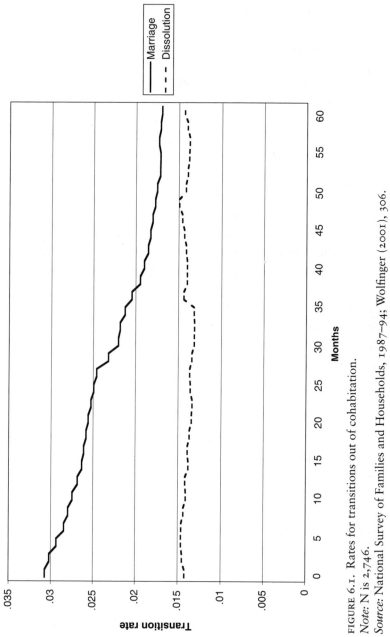

FIGURE 6.1. Rates for transitions out of cohabitation.
Note: N is 2,746.
Source: National Survey of Families and Households, 1987–94; Wolfinger (2001), 306.

If this is the case, then the children of divorce should be even more likely to dissolve their cohabiting relationships than they are to end their marriages. On the other hand, inherent instability may mean that the problematic interpersonal skills and reduced commitment responsible for the divorce cycle make less of a difference for cohabitation than they do for marriage: In the context of inherently unstable cohabiting relationships, those problems may lose their impact. This argument suggests that parental divorce should have minimal effects on the stability of cohabiting relationships.

Marriage is another way out of cohabitation. Chapter 3 shows that parental divorce often leads people to opt for cohabitation instead of marriage. Although the majority of cohabitors eventually wed, this may not hold true for the children of divorce, given their low overall marriage rates. Living with someone offers ample opportunity for problematic interpersonal skills to manifest themselves and discourage a move towards greater commitment.

How Parental Divorce Affects Cohabiting Relationships

I study cohabitation using data from both waves of the National Survey of Families and Households using the same analytic strategy I used for marital stability. Multiple parental family structure transitions should make cohabiting relationships more likely to dissolve and less likely to end in marriage. Stepparenting should exacerbate the effects of parental divorce. Socioeconomic differences between both respondents and their families of origin should have little to no effect on the relationship between family of origin and how cohabiting partnerships turn out. In short, the same patterns that characterize marriage also should hold true for cohabiting unions – although the magnitude may differ, given that cohabitation is a totally different kind of relationship.

These predictions almost uniformly turned out to be wrong, as Figure 6.2 shows. Parental divorce increases by only 15 percent the chances that an offspring's cohabiting relationship will dissolve, and this is not statistically significant. It is surprising that the relationship between family structure of origin and cohabitation stability

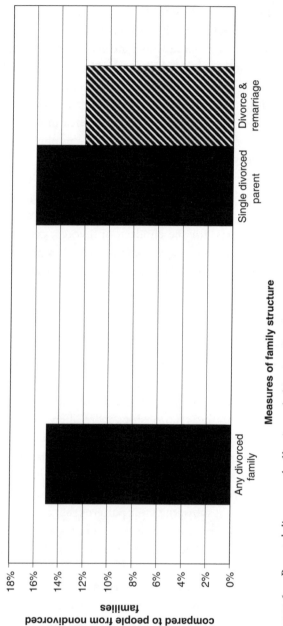

Measures of family structure

FIGURE 6.2. Parental divorce and offspring cohabitation dissolution.
Notes: N is 2,747. Analyses control for race, religion, gender of primary respondent, presence of siblings, birth cohort, and century month the cohabiting union began. Results are not statistically significant.
Source: National Survey of Families and Households, 1987–94.

is so weak, given that the minimum effect of parental divorce on offspring marital stability is about 50 percent. Furthermore, stepparenting makes the effects of parental divorce smaller, not larger. Experiencing three or more family structure transitions, which is associated with particularly high rates of divorce transmission, does not produce a high rate of cohabitation dissolution. Finally, socioeconomic differences between respondents have almost no effect on the relationship between parental divorce and the likelihood of dissolving a cohabiting relationship.

Parental divorce has a much stronger effect on the chances that cohabiting unions will end in wedlock. Figure 6.3 shows that the children of divorce are 21 percent less likely to marry a live-in partner than are people from intact families, a finding that makes sense given what we have learned in previous chapters: People from divorced families now have much lower marriage rates than people continuously raised by two parents. Parental divorce often leaves offspring with ambivalent feelings about marriage, due to the unpleasant experiences most of them have growing up. The children of divorce also are disproportionately likely to develop interpersonal skills not conducive to marital stability, and given the chance to emerge in a live-in relationship, these problems may discourage marriage.[15]

The relationship between parental divorce and the chances of marrying a cohabiting partner cannot be explained by sociodemographic differences, either between respondents or their families of origin. It is especially noteworthy that educational attainment, a strong predictor of marital stability, has almost no effect on the outcome of cohabiting relationships. I will return to this surprising finding, because it sheds light on the relationship between parental divorce and cohabitation stability.

The story becomes more complicated when the effects of stepparenting are taken into account, as Figure 6.3 shows. Parental remarriage completely offsets the negative effect of parental divorce on the chances a cohabiting relationship will end in wedlock. Thus people from stepfamilies are as likely to marry their cohabiting partners as are people from intact families, whereas offspring whose divorced

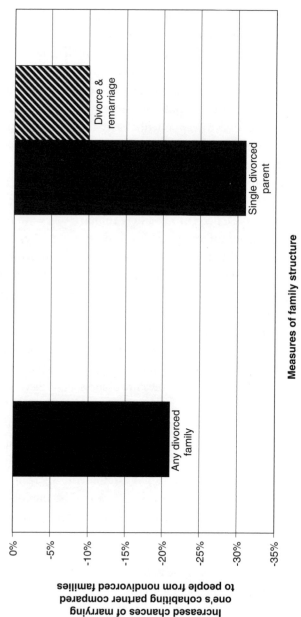

Measures of family structure

FIGURE 6.3. Parental divorce and the transition from cohabitation to marriage.
Note: N is 2,747. Analyses control for race, religion, gender of primary respondent, presence of siblings, birth cohort, and century month the cohabiting union began. Results for divorce and remarriage are not statistically significant.
Source: National Survey of Families and Households, 1987–94.

parents did not remarry are 31 percent less likely to marry their cohabiting partners.

These findings can be understood by reconsidering a discounted explanation for the effects of parental divorce. The role model theory attributes the divorce cycle to the absence of the parental role model necessary for learning the skills to succeed in a romantic relationship. Perhaps the most important evidence against the role model theory is the finding that parental remarriage increases the likelihood that the children of divorce will dissolve their own marriages. Nevertheless, role modeling can probably explain why parental remarriage offsets the effects of parental divorce on the chances that cohabiting partners will get married.

Stepparenting often restores children's faith in the institution of marriage.[16] Even if life in a stepfamily falls short of expectations, children may still come to accept marriage as a normal part of life. They may appreciate how remarriage benefitted their biological parents. Conversely, these children have less opportunity to cultivate an appreciation for single parenting: Life without a partner must not be that great (they may reason) or else my parent would have remained single. For these reasons, a stepparent may provide a role model for matrimony and thereby offset the large negative effect that parental divorce has on the likelihood that cohabiting partners will marry each other. Note that stepparenting produces expectations that are discrepant with reality: Although stepparenting increases the chances of getting married, it decreases the chances of staying married.

This seeming contradiction tells us a lot about how the children of divorce behave in cohabiting relationships. Remember that the children of divorce often have trouble in their own marriages because of reduced commitment and problematic interpersonal skills. Stepparenting only makes things worse, judging by stepchildren's higher divorce rate. So why doesn't stepparenting decrease the marriage rate for cohabiting relationships? After all, a partner with poor interpersonal skills should logically seem like a bad bet for marriage. Furthermore, why is there such a weak relationship between family background and the probability of dissolving a cohabiting relationship?

The answers have to do with the nature of cohabiting relationships. Recall that any cohabiting relationship is equally likely to end at any time, regardless of length. If cohabiting unions inherently lack stability, then the impaired interpersonal skills that sometimes result from parental divorce may make less difference than they do in marriage – they lose their importance in the context of inherently unstable unions.[17] In other words, live-in partnerships simply have too many destabilizing factors already working against them for parental divorce (a huge disadvantage in marriage) to compromise the stability of the union. By the time the problematic interpersonal skills resulting from parental divorce manifest themselves, the relationship probably already has dissolved of its own accord. It is additional evidence for this proposition that most of the sociodemographic variables that predict marital dissolution have almost no impact on cohabitation stability. Even relationships begun by teenagers do not have disproportionately high breakup rates, a finding strongly at odds with research on the link between marriage timing and divorce.[18]

Similar logic may explain why stepparenting does not reduce the chances that a cohabiting relationship will end in marriage. Recall that the odds of marriage are highest soon after two partners move in together. Couples may marry before problems resulting from impaired interpersonal skills have had time to manifest themselves.

Conclusion

Cohabitation has become commonplace. As marriage rates decline, live-in partnerships increasingly make up the difference. Many people who eventually will marry start by living together. These trends are especially pronounced for the children of divorce, who came of age when cohabitation rates began to increase. This historical connection underscores the relationship between parental divorce and cohabitation stability.

The nature of the relationship between parental divorce and offspring cohabitation emphasizes the differences between offspring cohabitation and marriage. Parental divorce has almost no effect on the odds that offspring will dissolve a cohabiting union, compared with the odds they will end a marriage. The children of divorce are somewhat less likely than people from intact families to marry their cohabiting partners, but still the effect is small compared to the relationship between parental divorce and offspring marital stability. It is not surprising that parental divorce decreases the chances of marrying one's cohabiting partner, given the low overall marriage rate of the children of divorce. The greater mystery is why parental divorce has so little effect on the chances of dissolving a cohabiting union.

There are both empirical and theoretical answers. Empirically, we must look to the inherent instability of cohabiting relationships. In a relationship that can break up at any time, the disadvantages conferred by parental divorce make little difference. Nor, apparently, does anything else. Strong predictors of divorce such as age at marriage and educational attainment have essentially no effect on the stability of cohabiting relationships. This is additional evidence for the argument that the nature of cohabitation makes family background unimportant.

The theoretical answer highlights today's young people as unique in the recent history of intimate relationships: Cohabitation, we might argue is theirs and theirs alone. Marriage is what our forebears did, they might say, and look where it got them: Fifty-fifty chances – essentially even money – that a new union would fail. So young people, many of them children of divorce turn their backs on marriage in small but growing numbers to focus on *their* relationship, the one their generation brought into vogue. And in cohabiting relationships the traditional disadvantages, such as parental divorce, do not matter at all.

This is only speculation. Nevertheless, the simultaneous rise of divorce and cohabitation is striking, as has been the media attention heralding Generation X's rejection of traditional values. Perhaps this can help explain why the children of divorce behave so differently in cohabiting relationships than they do in marriage.

In any event, it may be too soon to come to any firm conclusions. The rise of cohabitation in American society has made living with a partner out of wedlock a different experience. Cohabiting relationships have become less stable in recent years, with higher dissolution rates and fewer couples getting married. Larry Bumpass and Hsien-Hen Lu have attributed these developments to the increased acceptability of cohabitation, leading more people with casual relationships to live together.[19] If cohabitation continues to be less stable than marriage, then we can expect the effects of family structure on these two kinds of relationship to remain different. The effects of family structure on cohabitation should only grow stronger if cohabitation becomes more like marriage.

SEVEN

Conclusion

ALTHOUGH DIVORCE RATES have dipped since the record highs of the late 1970s, they remain higher than at any other time in American history. All of the conditions responsible for the divorce boom are likely to persist for the foreseeable future: A mass exodus of women from the workplace hardly can be imagined; people will continue to feel entitled to escape unhappy marriages; and it is highly unlikely that American standards of living will regress to pre-1950s levels – which would preclude divorce by making it more difficult to live by oneself. There is no reason to expect that rates ever will return to the levels of the 1950s.

The declines in divorce of the past twenty-five years portend the magnitude of any future changes in the divorce rate. Fluctuations in relative cohort size and the economy may bring about change, but as history has shown, any effect on the divorce rate is likely to be temporary. Events similar to the demobilization of servicemen after World War II could precipitate brief but acute spikes in the divorce rate. There is a greater point to be made here: The 1965–79 divorce boom represented the culmination of a trend that extended back hundreds of years – that is, as far back as divorce rates have been recorded. Perhaps the only thing that could drive down divorce rates would be drastic legal measures. Although ill-advised, legislative responses to the divorce "problem" are not entirely implausible. The findings presented in this book speak to the issue of divorce law, so I will return to it later in this chapter.

Few people react neutrally to the subject of divorce. Some are enthusiastic proponents, because to them divorce represents the hitherto unknown freedom (particularly for women) to leave unfulfilling or abusive marriages. For its proponents, the divorce revolution represents victory after centuries of struggle against a restrictive society. At the other end of the spectrum are those who see divorce as abhorrent. As it is for the enthusiasts, divorce is viewed by its detractors as a barometer of moral and social trends, but their interpretation is very different. They see divorce as synonymous with the breakdown of the family and, accordingly, traditional values. Most people have beliefs lying somewhere between these positions; in other words, divorce is a necessary evil, sometimes unpleasant or injurious to the participants but preferable to the continuation of an untenable marriage.[1]

Until recently, most arguments for and against divorce have been largely speculative. With the advent of modern social science it became possible to address these issues more concretely, and the high divorce rate provided the impetus to do so. We are now far enough from the divorce boom to understand its consequences for adults and children.

This book confirms that the divorce cycle is an integral part of the demographic landscape in contemporary America. Growing up in a divorced family greatly increases the chances that one's own marriage will end in divorce. Although the magnitude of the increase varies, it is reasonable to say that compared to people who did not come from divorced families, experiencing parental divorce increases the chances of ending one's own marriage by at least 50 percent.

Over the past few decades, researchers have demonstrated that gender, religion, race, and socioeconomic origins have considerable ability to explain social behavior. As a phenomenon with implications for the social science, the divorce cycle is extraordinarily powerful, because it operates largely irrespective of all these demographic influences: Parental divorce affects members of different groups the same way. Moreover, family structure of origin is a stronger predictor of offspring marital stability than are religion, race, or socioeconomic background.[2]

These are significant results given the ubiquity of divorce in contemporary America. About 40 percent of children will grow up in divorced families; hence, many millions of adults will experience the effects of divorce on their own marital behavior in profound ways.[3]

Parental Divorce and Offspring Marital Behavior:
A Life Span Chronology

Parental divorce affects every important aspect of offspring behavior in intimate relationships: marriage timing; partner selection; the stability of first and subsequent marriages; and behavior in nonmarital cohabiting relationships. In the following pages I describe how the findings presented in this book collectively influence offspring behavior across the life course.

Marriage Timing

Evidence of the divorce cycle begins early in the life course. Parental divorce increases the incidence of premature teenage sexual activity, which in turn leads to teenage marriage. Another reason the children of divorce have high rates of teenage marriage is their desire to escape unhappy home lives. At age eighteen, for instance, 1994 General Social Survey (GSS) respondents from divorced families have marriage rates 27 percent higher than their peers from intact families. Generally, teenagers in stepfamilies have marriage rates about 20 percent higher than do those whose divorced parents did not remarry. The effect of parental divorce on offspring marital behavior diminishes as the children of divorce leave their teens, so that by age twenty the children of divorce have marriage rates comparable to people from intact families.

The relationship between parental divorce and teenage marriage has important implications for marital stability. Other things being equal, a couple with a mean marriage age of twenty is 32 percent less likely to divorce than a couple with a mean marriage age of eighteen.[4] Most teenagers are not ready for a commitment as serious and potentially enduring as matrimony. The longer they wait, the more likely they are to develop the social and inner resources necessary to succeed in their marriages. The propensity for youthful wedlock therefore contributes to the difficulties the children of divorce face in their own marriages, although it is far from being the most important cause of the divorce cycle. People who delay marriage also are more likely to graduate from college.[5] Youthful marriage often forces newlyweds into the work force or into duty as homemakers.

If the children of divorce do not marry by age twenty, the likelihood of their ever marrying dips about 30 percent below that of their peers from intact families. Growing up in a divorced family often leaves offspring ambivalent about marriage. Many opt for cohabitation, a form of intimate relationship offering some of the same benefits of marriage but not entailing the same commitment or risk.

This is a mixed blessing. Cohabitation inherently is a less stable form of union than matrimony, with lower levels of partner satisfaction. On the other hand, judging by their high divorce rates, some people from divorced families may not be suited for marriage. If they cohabit instead, they spare themselves, their partners, and possibly their children the upheaval of divorce. Finally, it should not be forgotten that many people who cohabit will eventually marry each other. Parental divorce plays a role here too; I will say more about that later in this chapter.

Mate Selection

Parental divorce affects not only the decision to marry but the kinds of people chosen as spouses. In particular, the children of divorce often marry other children of divorce, a phenomenon I have called family structure homogamy. Compared to people from intact families, the children of divorce are about 50 percent more likely to choose a spouse from a divorced family. This helps explain the divorce cycle, given that marriages between people from divorced families are more likely to fail than are unions involving only one child of divorce.

Even more than the divorce cycle itself, family structure homogamy affects everybody the same way, transcending barriers of gender, race, religion, and to a large extent social class. Variations in family structure such as parental remarriage and multiple parental divorces have no effect on the chances of choosing a spouse from a divorced family. The only personal characteristic that affects family structure homogamy is education. People with college degrees are considerably less likely to marry the children of divorce, a result that probably can be explained on the basis of marriage markets. Parental divorce decreases the chances of attending college. Thus the children of divorce are underrepresented on any given college campus, while many people who attend college will meet their future spouses there. This reduces the likelihood that college graduates will marry people from divorced families. Even after accounting for differences in education, the children of divorce are likely to marry other children of divorce, so college attendance plays only a partial role in explaining the relationship between parental background and partner selection.

More generally, family structure homogamy tells us something important about the long-term consequences of family breakdown. Parental divorce clearly has far-reaching effects on offspring if such a broad demographic variable – family structure – can exert such a great influence on something so deeply personal: the kind of person one chooses to marry. In this regard, family structure homogamy is one of the deeper mysteries described in this book. Although the psychological mechanisms responsible for the divorce cycle are fairly well understood, it is not clear why people from divorced families are so likely to marry other children of divorce. Perhaps in-depth clinical interviews or survey data with detailed psychometric information could shed light on the subject.

What Makes the Divorce Cycle Stronger? Or Weaker?

Family structure homogamy helps explain the divorce cycle. If both spouses come from divorced families, the marriage becomes over 200 percent more likely to fail than a marriage between people who did not grow up in divorced families. This result accords with the finding that divorce transmission can be attributed to reduced marital commitment. It makes sense that a marriage where both spouses exhibit low commitment is more likely to fail than a union where only one or neither spouse exhibits reduced commitment. In colloquial terms, there simply is less glue to hold the relationship together. This is important to keep in mind given the high likelihood that the children of divorce will marry each other.

Another important variable affecting the strength of divorce transmission concerns the number of family structure transitions children undergo while growing up. Other things being equal, the rate of divorce transmission increases with each disruption. The divorce cycle is set into motion initially when a child experiences divorce. The chances that the child will end a marriage increase considerably with parental remarriage, while a second parental divorce increases the probability even more.

In the past, when the divorce rate was lower, it was uncommon for children to experience multiple disruptions. The average respondent to the National Survey of Families and Households (NSFH) analyzed in this book was born in the late 1940s. Only about 1 percent experienced three or more family structure transitions while growing up. In contrast, approximately 20 percent of children born in the late 1970s experienced at least three disruptions, a figure almost *twenty times* higher than for the 1940s respondents.[6] Since each disruption increases the chances that adult offspring will have difficulty in their own marriages, the declining rate of divorce transmission described in Chapter 5 is all the more remarkable.

Because they strengthen the message children receive about low commitment, multiple transitions while growing up increase the likelihood of divorce transmission. A child who experiences one divorce may learn that marriage need not last forever. After a second divorce, the message becomes clearer. Stepparenting probably reinforces this message by suggesting that spouses can be replaced.

This last point is speculative. Most studies have shown that remarriage exacerbates the negative effects of parental divorce (or at the very least has no impact on children), so the results described here accord with previous research on the consequences of stepparenting. Moreover, the effects of stepparenting on offspring marital behavior can easily be interpreted within the framework established by the "low commitment" explanation for the divorce cycle: The presence of a stepparent shows children that divorce does not mean forever forsaking marriage. Perhaps for this reason, offspring raised in stepfamilies have even higher divorce rates than do people raised in single-parent divorced families.

Multiple transitions while growing up affect second and third marriages as well as initial unions. This finding is interesting for two reasons. First, the children of divorce do not change their marital behavior as a result of their experiences in their initial marriages; the adverse consequences of parental divorce apparently manifest themselves in all of one's conjugal relationships. Second, people's marital behavior mirrors their childhood experiences. The more marital transitions children experience, the more marriages they are likely to dissolve as adults. This provides a useful template for understanding the divorce cycle, and perhaps other patterns of adult behavior that occur consequent to growing up in a divorced family. It also is evidence for a fundamentally simple understanding of human behavior: We repeat what we learn in our youth.

Parental divorce affects offspring marital behavior largely irrespective of social differences between offspring and their families of origin. Parental socioeconomic characteristics – education, occupation, history of receiving public aid – as well as offspring marriage timing account for a small portion of the relationship between growing up in a divorced family and one's own marital stability. Perhaps the most important demographic variable affecting the divorce cycle is education, given the effect of parental divorce on educational attainment and the strong correlation between education and marital stability. Combined, parental socioeconomic status, respondent education, marriage age, and other demographic differences between people from divorced and intact families account for at best one-third of the divorce cycle. Most of the remainder is attributable, as Paul Amato and others have shown, to the effects of parental divorce on marital functioning and commitment.[7]

The "black box" explanation for divorce transmission is genetics, but its role in the divorce cycle cannot be ascertained with the data at hand. It could not be preponderant, though, given that the divorce cycle has many nonbiological determinants. If the divorce cycle were completely attributable to genetics, social differences between respondents (such as education or the presence of stepparents) would not produce different levels of divorce transmission. Genetics also cannot explain why the negative effects of parental divorce have weakened over time.

Historical Trends

Increases in the divorce rate have diminished the negative consequences of coming from a divorced family. Two phenomena have been affected: the divorce cycle itself; and the association between family background and marriage timing.

Teenagers from divorced families still have higher marriage rates than do teenagers from intact families, but the gap narrowed between 1973 and 1994. The most likely explanation for this trend concerns the changing circumstances under which people choose to divorce. In the absence of no-fault divorce laws, couples needed greater justification to obtain a divorce. When couples finally ended their marriages, the situation may have deteriorated much further than is typical in most modern divorces. It is impossible to know for certain whether only the very worst marriages were dissolved in years gone by. But if we accept this proposition, it follows that children used to be exposed to far more conflict than is typical in most modern divorces. One reason that teenagers from divorced families married was to escape unpleasant home environments. If parental divorce is less unpleasant than it used to be, teenagers may feel less pressure to escape through marriage. This could explain why their marriage rates have been lower in recent years.

As Chapter 2 showed, many of the negative consequences of growing up in a divorced family (excluding the divorce cycle) can be linked to parental conflict, so declining conflict may have indirectly reduced the rate of teenage marriage. The children of divorce often become sexually active as teenagers, and premature sexual activity increases the chances of early wedlock. Thus a decline in parental conflict may have benefitted the children of divorce by reducing the early sexual activity that would ultimately lead to high rates of teenage pregnancy and marriage.

Past age twenty, the children of divorce now have lower overall marriage rates, whereas thirty years ago the opposite was true. The most likely explanation for this development is the increased acceptability of cohabitation as an alternative to matrimony. Growing up in a divorced family often reduces children's faith in the institution of marriage, so they cohabit instead. As cohabitation grew more common, it became an increasingly appealing option for the children of divorce.

The declining rate of teenage marriage has contributed to the weakening of the divorce cycle. Since youthful marriage is a strong predictor of divorce, the children of divorce now fare better in their own marriages because they are less likely to wed as teenagers. General Social Survey respondents from divorced single-parent families interviewed in 1973 were 126 percent more likely to have dissolved their own marriages than were people from intact families. By 1994, the disparity had declined to 45 percent. Controlling for age at marriage reduces the figures for 1973 and 1994 to 94 percent and 33 percent, respectively. The divorce cycle would have abated even if rates of teenage marriage had not declined, although changing patterns of marriage timing have had a substantial impact.

Rates of divorce transmission have not changed for people raised in stepfamilies. Between 1973 and 1994, GSS respondents experiencing both parental divorce and remarriage were 91 percent more likely to end their own marriages than were people from intact families.

The divorce cycle is primarily attributable to the effect of parental divorce on marital commitment, and the message children receive about commitment has almost certainly changed over time. If your parents were the only couple in the neighborhood to end their marriage – a fairly common situation prior to the 1960s – it conveyed a far more poignant lesson about the permanence of marital bonds than it does today. Children learned that marriage could be forsaken when it went sour, and that sometimes the best solution to marital difficulties was to cut one's losses and move on. In contrast, no matter how painful it is at the time, a modern divorce does not stand out against the experiences of one's peers, and therefore does not send nearly as strong a message to offspring about commitment. Surrounded by divorced families, today's children learn relatively similar lessons about marital commitment whether or not their own parents are divorced. As a result, people are now less likely to divorce as a result of growing up in a divorced family. The normalization of divorce, in short, means that it conveys a weaker message about marital commitment than it once did.

The declining stigma of growing up in a divorced family probably also has contributed to lower rates of divorce transmission. In the past, when divorces were few and far between, single mothers and their children were often viewed with both contempt and pity. Under these conditions, the children were less likely to develop normal relationships with their peers, relatives, and communities. This may have exacerbated the lessons children learned about marital commitment, given the powerful relationship between stigma and personal development, and increased their chances of having difficulty in their own marriages.

Historical data on stigma and marital commitment are not available. It is impossible to verify these explanations for the weakening of the divorce cycle, but they do accord with what historians have told us about the nature of divorce in years gone by. Moreover, various studies (cited in Chapter 5) confirm that the negative consequences of growing up in a divorced family have declined over time.

Even if the reasons for the weakening in the divorce cycle cannot be verified, the implications are undeniable: Declines in the intergenerational transmission of divorce mean that millions of young Americans now face substantially lower odds of divorce in their own marriages than they would have, had the rates of divorce transmission remained constant. In addition, rates of teenage marriage for the children of divorce also have declined. Fewer teenage marriages by the children of divorce diminishes the number of at-risk unions, and should in itself contribute to lower divorce rates. Irrespective of whether they persist, these trends have transformed our demographic landscape for decades to come. All else being equal, a lower rate of divorce transmission in this generation means fewer divorces in the next.

Parental Divorce and Offspring Cohabiting Relationships

Another change in the American family has been higher rates of non-marital cohabitation. Given that people from divorced families disproportionately are likely to live with their partners out of wedlock, it is important to understand how parental divorce affects these relationships. The answers presented in Chapter 6 are at odds with the rest of this book. Growing up in a divorced family has almost no effect on the likelihood of dissolving a cohabiting relationship. This probably can be attributed to the fundamental instability of these unions. Within a partnership that is likely to break up at any time anyway, the low commitment to intimate relationships frequently evinced by the children of divorce seems to make little difference. By the time low commitment manifests itself, the cohabiting relationship may have dissolved of its own accord.

Parental divorce decreases the chances of marrying one's cohabiting partner by about 20 percent. This result is consistent with the low overall marriage rate for the children of divorce. If interpersonal difficulties and low levels of commitment are responsible for the divorce cycle, they also should discourage cohabiting partners from marrying each other. Cohabiting relationships provide ample opportunity for interpersonal difficulties and low commitment to manifest themselves. With this in mind, it is surprising that parental remarriage completely offsets the negative relationship between growing up in a divorced family and the likelihood of marrying one's cohabiting partner. People from stepfamilies, in other words, are as likely to marry their cohabiting partners as are people from intact families.

Remarriage often restores in children a faith in marriage that had been compromised by parental divorce. This may explain why stepchildren and people from intact families are equally likely to marry their cohabiting partners. But this restored faith often turns out to be illusory, given that parental remarriage greatly increases the chances of having difficulty in one's own marriage. Still, the effect of parental remarriage on offspring cohabiting relationships is noteworthy, in that it runs contrary to almost every other finding on the divorce cycle – findings that uniformly show that remarriage exacerbates the negative effects of parental divorce.

Taken together, the results presented in this book contribute to a growing body of literature on the differences between marriage and cohabitation.[8]

Limitations

The results reported in this book have two specific limitations. First, I study behavior only in heterosexual unions. Adequate data do not exist yet to study gay and lesbian partnerships, which are less common than their heterosexual counterparts – and perhaps, less likely to be acknowledged. A national sample survey, even if very large, produces only minute numbers of gay and lesbian unions. The NSFH sample of over 13,000 people yields about ten respondents in same-sex live-in partnerships. Perhaps future research will produce an adequate sample of same-sex partnerships.[9]

A second limitation concerns generalizability. This book is about the divorce cycle in the United States; its findings should be applied to other countries with caution. Research has confirmed the divorce cycle in England, France, the Netherlands, and Germany, so it is entirely possible that the cycle occurs in all countries where the process of divorce is to some degree Westernized.[10]

The Divorce Reform Movement in America

In recent years, many people have identified high divorce rates as a social problem that threatens America. It is well known that divorce often has numerous negative consequences for parents and children alike. No-fault divorce laws frequently have been blamed for the divorce boom that took place between 1965 and 1979, despite considerable evidence to the contrary.[11] The most commonly proposed solution to America's "divorce problem" is to repeal or weaken no-fault laws, thereby preserving more intact families and reducing the societal ills attributed to high divorce rates.

Concern with high divorce rates and "family breakdown" is by no means only a modern phenomenon. By the 1860s, divorce law had become more liberal than ever before, although the acceptable grounds for marital dissolution varied widely across states.[12] Divorce has increased steadily since the Civil War, when rates could be tracked reliably for the first time. The *casus belli* for opponents of divorce – rising divorce rates coupled with easier divorce laws – were therefore in place, with predictable results. In 1867, for example, Yale University president Theodore Woolsey denounced "corruption in the family, as manifested by connubial unfaithfulness and divorce." Americans' destiny, he continued, "depends on our ability to keep family life pure and simple."[13] The beginning of the twentieth century witnessed a spate of anti-divorce activism, with more than 100 pieces of restrictive legislation passed by state governments.[14]

With the 1965–79 divorce boom exceeding any other in American history, it is little surprise that attention has turned once again to the question of divorce reform. One difference from previous efforts concerns the invocation of sophisticated social science research. Whereas turn-of-the-century condemnation of high divorce rates resorted to moral arguments,[15] modern divorce reformers base their proposals on hard data: Marital disruption often has devastating effects on women's incomes and offspring well-being.[16] This provided the ammunition activists and politicians could use to push divorce reform forward. Rep. Tony Perkins, sponsor of the Louisiana Covenant Marriage law, made this point in a 1997 interview:

> Well, legislatures around the country are continually dealing with issues trying to create new laws to address teenage pregnancy, juvenile delinquency...a number of these issues. And now what social science is telling us is that these issues trace right back to broken homes.[17]

The timing was right for a resurgence in public condemnation of divorce. No-fault laws had been in place for some time when the divorce reform movement reappeared in the 1990s, providing policy makers with ample opportunity to capitalize on the putative consequences of divorce depicted in the work of Judith Wallerstein, Lenore Weitzman, and others. Their research spurred on conservative activists; divorce reform legislation was introduced in over thirty states in the 1990s.[18] Language urging the reconsideration of no-fault divorce appeared in the 2000 Republican Party Platform.[19]

Most of the state-level efforts at divorce reform have failed. The first success did not come until 1997, with passage of the Louisiana Covenant Marriage law. Similar legislation was enacted in Arizona in the following year, followed by Arkansas in 2001.[20] All three measures created two-tiered marriage systems: Couples could opt for either traditional unions, which were dissolvable under no-fault statutes, or covenant marriage. The latter effectively reintroduced fault-based divorce law; petitioners have to prove adultery, abuse, or similarly egregious conduct. In the absence of such transgressions, couples have to separate for one or more years before a divorce decree could be granted. Furthermore, counseling must be sought prior to obtaining a divorce. Of the three states, Arizona's covenant marriage law is the most liberal. Fault-based statutes or prolonged separation only apply if one spouse contests the divorce.

Covenant marriage has not caught on so far. In 1998, less than 2 percent of Louisiana newlyweds opted for covenant marriages.[21] These unions do appear to have lower divorce rates, although the difference is largely due to the fact that only couples less prone to ending their relationships are likely to choose the covenant option in the first place. In particular, wives in covenant marriages are likely to have religious beliefs that discourage divorce.[22] Even if divorce rates are lower, covenant marriage laws may not have reduced the suffering attributed to divorce. One potentially adverse consequence of making divorce difficult to obtain is to trap children in damaging, high-conflict marriages. I will return to this topic later.

Despite its apparent lack of appeal in Louisiana, divorce reformers have not given up on covenant marriage. It appeared in the plank offered in 2000 by the Marriage Movement, an eclectic group of clergy, scholars, and state politicians. Attracting national attention, the movement offers numerous ideas for strengthening marriage.[23]

One of these is covenant marriage; another is proposed legislation to uniformly weaken no-fault laws:

> Reconsider no-fault divorce laws and find innovative new ways to give legal weight to the marriage vow. For example, a longer waiting period (at least eighteen months for contested no-fault divorces), slows down the divorce process. . . .[24]

Given the thousands of academics, theologians, public officials, and concerned citizens listed as signatories to its mission statement, the marriage movement exemplifies American concern with divorce. Inspired by such broad-based support, some of the divorce reform legislation now under consideration may well become law.

Although many people feel the divorce rate in contemporary America is too high, not all agree that tougher divorce laws are a good way to preserve marriage. Some have argued that more families best can be kept together through governmental programs that make life easier for married couples.[25] The scope of ideas is extensive, ranging from increased financial assistance for low-income married couples to government-sponsored training in relationship skills.[26] Some programs already have been implemented. Recently, the federal tax burden incurred by low-income married couples was reduced, while certain states have begun marriage education programs.

Do these programs help keep marriages together? For the most part it is too soon to tell.[27] One mark in their favor is that they can't hurt. People may object to government-subsidized marital education as a waste of taxpayers' money or an unwarranted intrusion into people's private lives. It is hard to imagine, though, that the newlyweds learning about happy marriages actually might be harmed in the process – as long as governmental agencies do not use marriage programs as an excuse to curtail more vital services.[28] On the other hand, as I will contend in the following pages, the discouraging legacy of tough divorce laws is hardly in question.

Though not formally associated with the marriage movement, one auspicious development in all fifty states has been the elevation of the minimum marriage age to eighteen. Until recently, for example, women could wed at fifteen in Mississippi. Given the high divorce rates for teenagers chronicled earlier in this book – and the high rates of teenage marriage for the children of divorce – the prohibition of youthful marriage eventually may contribute to lower divorce rates.

In many states, the legal minimum marriage age of eighteen can be waived by parental or judicial consent, or by premarital pregnancy. Marriage between teenagers may be desirable when babies are involved, but the merits of youthful marriage via parental or judicial approval seem suspect. This is a potential area for legal reform on the part of the marriage movement. In addition, we might do more to discourage matrimony among eighteen- and nineteen-year-olds. As of 2000, about 5 percent of American teenagers were married.[29] Perhaps marriage education programs might seek to persuade teenagers to delay marriage until their twenties, given the high divorce risk youthful couples face.

The Argument for No-Fault Laws

The results presented in this book comprise strong evidence for the proposition that eliminating no-fault divorce laws would be harmful to the children of divorce. The negative effects of growing up in a divorced family have abated, essentially because divorce became more common. The reintroduction of tough divorce laws might well revive many of the conditions that used to make divorce harder on children. Although fewer children might experience broken homes if no-fault laws were weakened or abrogated, their suffering would increase.

The normalization of divorce has benefitted children in various ways. Lower rates of teenage marriage for the children of divorce reduce the likelihood that they will have difficulties in their own marriages. As we saw earlier in this chapter, a couple with a mean marriage age of twenty is 32 percent less likely to divorce than one with a mean marriage age of eighteen. People who marry young also are less likely to remain in school. Furthermore, the weakening divorce cycle means that fewer children of divorce will end their own marriages than would otherwise be the case.

Recall that divorce used to be far more stigmatized than it is today. The stigma of divorce would revive if couples once more had to demonstrate legal fault in order to dissolve their marriages. Under these conditions, parental divorce would again send children a stronger message about marital commitment than it does now, thereby increasing the chances that they will end their own marriages. This might well raise the overall divorce rate for future generations.

If no-fault laws were repealed, many parents would wait longer before dissolving disastrous marriages. The children involved would be subjected to far more conflict than is typical in most modern divorces. As we have seen, parental conflict takes a heavy toll on children. In particular, it may push them into teenage marriages. Thus the reintroduction of tough divorce laws almost certainly would raise rates of youthful matrimony by encouraging teenagers to escape acrimony at home.

Supporters of covenant marriage might respond that domestic abuse is one of the stipulated grounds for fault. Be that as it may, much of the parental conflict so harmful to children falls short of actual violence. For truly violent marriages, the need to demonstrate fault probably would dissuade many prospective divorcées who would otherwise leave their abusive partners more quickly.

Critics of easy divorce laws might question the findings presented in this book. Some already have done so. In a *Los Angeles Times* editorial, Norval Glenn and David Blankenhorn expressed doubt that the declining rate of divorce transmission has benefitted children.[30] Some of their objection pertains to media misrepresentation, rather than what I actually said. The divorce rate for the children of divorce did not decline between 1973 and 1994, as some newspapers reported. Glenn and Blankenhorn correctly identify my finding as a convergence in divorce rates for people from divorced and nondivorced families. I see this as evidence of a decline in the negative effects of divorce on children; they view it as "entirely the result of a remarkable increase in divorce-proneness in recent decades of U.S. adults who were raised in intact families." Divorce rates certainly increased over time for people from both divorced and intact families.

The primary causes of the divorce boom – women in the workplace, the increased acceptability of leaving a troubled marriage – affected everyone, irrespective of family background. Glenn and Blankenhorn seemed to acknowledge this point (and contradict their earlier statement about the divorce-proneness of people from intact families) when they went on to say, "In a high-divorce society, *everyone's* marriage is made weaker [emphasis added]." This may well be true, but it does not negate the declining contribution that parental divorce makes to the overall divorce rate. If my results reflected only the weakening of marriage, the disparity in marriage rates between people from divorced and nondivorced families would not have diminished over time.

Opponents of easy divorce often cite the grim economic condition of single mothers as a reason to justify stringent divorce laws. The Louisiana covenant marriage legislation was motivated in part by the economic consequences of divorce.[31] Indeed, poverty rates for single-mother families traditionally have been five times those of two-parent families.[32] But this, too, has changed. Although divorced women still suffer economically, their median income losses after divorce have declined significantly in recent years. This can be attributed largely to women's progress in the workplace.

Between 1980 and 2000, the proportion of women with college degrees rose from 13 percent to 24 percent; with high school diplomas, from 66 percent to 84 percent. Over the same time period, married women's labor force participation increased from 50 percent to 61 percent.[33] Women employed during marriage have more work experience should their marriages end, and experience enables divorced women to earn higher wages. These and other developments have improved divorced women's economic prospects: NSFH data show that marital dissolution now has a smaller economic effect on women than it did in the past. Divorce now costs the median woman 14 percent of her per capita income – considerably less than the 23–25 percent estimates based on data from the 1970s to the mid 1980s.[34] To be sure, a 14 percent loss in per capita income still represents a decline in quality of life, but this figure may shrink further as women's labor force prospects continue to improve.

It should go without saying that both single mothers and their children fare better when not left impoverished by divorce. For instance, income deprivation accounts for up to 50 percent of the relationship between parental divorce and offspring failure to graduate from high school.[35] In conjunction with the diminishing negative consequences of growing up in a divorced family, the improvement in divorcées' economic well-being undercuts a key rationale of the divorce reform movement. Why restrict divorce, ostensibly to protect women and children, when the economic reasons for doing so are weaker than ever before?

The final reasons for rejecting fault-based divorce are moral. Consider the charade spouses endured to sue for divorce on grounds of adultery, often when there had been no such conduct.[36] The usual practice was to hire a professional "co-respondent," nominally an adulterer, along with a photographer. Compromising photographs coupled with false testimony would then be presented in court to obtain a divorce decree. Everyone present was aware that the adultery may never have occurred. The tolerance of perjury is deplorable, but doubtless many perjurers felt those transgressions were outweighed by intolerable marital problems. Such was the state of affairs in the days before no-fault divorce, and such would be the state of affairs again if the critics of easy divorce laws have their way.

Tough divorce laws had other moral implications beside sham court proceedings. The traditional alternative to divorce, especially in the absence of adequate means to buy a trip to Reno, was permanent separation. Numerous unhappy couples effectively ended their marriages in this way. In the absence of a paper trail, it is impossible to know how many. Because most of those who opted for permanent separation did not want to spend the rest of their lives alone, adultery or even bigamy ensued. South Carolina stands out as an extreme example of the folly of prohibiting divorce. Having no divorce laws until fairly recently, South Carolina fostered peculiar conditions for marriage. In the mid-nineteenth century, laws had to be passed limiting the amount of money a man could bequeath to his mistress, given the popularity of engaging in extramarital relations in lieu of divorce.[37] Moreover, such arrangements offered no solution for the female half in such loveless marriages. By demonstrating one limit of legislating morality, these nineteenth-century laws are instructive to those who object to divorce on moral grounds.

Mixed Blessings

Although parental divorce no longer hurts children as much as it once did, it still has many negative consequences for offspring marital behavior. Moreover, some of the positive developments described in this book have had undesirable side effects. The first concerns the changing marital behavior of people from divorced families. Although lower rates of teenage marriage are certainly a welcome development, the other side of the coin has been lower marriage rates across the board for the children of divorce. Recall that GSS respondents from divorced families interviewed in 1973 had higher overall marriage rates than did people from intact families, owing largely to extraordinary levels of teenage marriage. By 1994, the children of divorce were 13 percent less likely to marry than were their peers from intact families, because they had low rates of matrimony past age twenty.

Doubtless many people who remain single throughout their lives are happy doing so, but marriage remains the normative experience for most of us; about 90 percent of Americans will wed at some point in their lives.[38] Furthermore, married people typically report greater emotional well-being than do those who remain single.[39] For many people, marriage is a wonderfully enriching experience, so it is of concern that an increasing number of people may be missing out on it because of their experiences while growing up. Cohabitation, often the preferred alternative for the children of divorce, sometimes provides the same benefits as marriage, but more often than not these relationships are short-lived. Perhaps at some point in the future this no longer will be the case, but for the time being the average duration of cohabiting relationships is declining.[40]

Another development that might be a mixed blessing for the children of divorce concerns the circumstances under which spouses choose to end their marriages. It is certainly good news that people are less likely to stay in high-conflict marriages than they used to be. However, it is also cause for concern if the majority of divorces come after virtually no conflict, given that ending a low-conflict marriage may hurt children as much as staying in a high-conflict family.[41] Recall from Chapter 2 that the odds of divorce transmission are highest if parents dissolve a marriage after little or no conflict.[42] In recent years this has been the case for a surprisingly large number of people: Paul Amato and Alan Booth have established that less than one-third of divorces occurring between 1980 and 1992 were preceded by serious conflict.[43] Although my findings indicate that the negative consequences of growing up in a divorced family have abated, Amato and Booth's result implies that declining levels of marital conflict ultimately may have adverse effects on offspring. Certainly there is a break-even point at which children's well-being is served best if their parent's marriage is dissolved. This is suggested by Amato and Booth's research, which identifies a middling level of conflict at which neither divorce nor continued marriage seems preferable for offspring.

Although growing up in a divorced family still has negative consequences for offspring well-being, this book has reported favorable developments in divorce demography – the declining negative effects of parental divorce on offspring marriage timing and duration. In contrast, Amato and Booth report a negative development: An increasing number of divorces take place after minimal levels of parental conflict, and low-conflict divorces hurt children. Nevertheless, Amato and Booth's research militates against the abolition of no-fault divorce. Tougher divorce laws would not allow children to escape rancorous marriages. This very likely is what happened in the past, and very likely what would happen in the future if access to divorce were restricted.

Paradoxically, the divorce boom has engendered social conditions that make divorce easier for children, but the story is far from uniformly positive. Growing up in a divorced family still has serious consequences for children's behavior in their own romantic relationships, and some generally beneficial developments – such as the trend toward later marriage – have had negative side effects. The divorce boom, in sum, has been a mixed blessing in these and numerous other respects. Researchers are still debating its implications. With this in mind, a cautious reading of the findings presented in this book might lead one to conclude that the family is in a state of change. Such a conclusion still provides a strong rationale for not weakening or abrogating no-fault divorce laws. A preponderance of change means that more change may be on the way. It also indicates that researchers and policy makers do not know the whole story, and they probably should know the whole story before turning back the calendar on divorce laws. Divorce is often bad for children, but eliminating no-fault divorce would be worse.

Data and Methods

Data

CHAPTER 6 ANALYZES data from the National Survey of Families and Households (NSFH), while Chapter 5 uses the General Social Survey (GSS). Chapters 3 and 4 employ both data sets. The NSFH contains unusually detailed measures of marital behavior and cohabitation, while the GSS provides trend data with a large aggregated sample size. No other data sets offer these features.

The NSFH is a national sample survey of adults nineteen and over in the United States.[1] The respondents interviewed in 1987 and 1988 numbered 13,007. This included a main sample of 9,643 respondents plus an oversample of minorities, newlyweds, single parents, individual parents in stepparent families, and individuals in cohabiting unions. From 1992 to 1994, 10,008 respondents were re-interviewed. This raises the question of whether to use both waves in order to maximize information on respondent relationship histories. However, analyzing only Wave One provides a larger overall sample size, as well as eliminating the possibility of attrition bias. I use both waves of data in the two analyses for which extensive information on relationship histories is especially desirable: the investigations of entire respondent marital histories (Chapter 4); and cohabitation stability (Chapter 6). Preliminary analyses suggested that respondent attrition is unlikely to have affected the results. Elsewhere I use only the Wave one data.

In addition to the primary interviews, current spouses of NSFH respondents were also queried. Information on former spouses and nonresponding current spouses was obtained from the primary respondents. Spousal data are used in Chapters 3 and 4.

Sample sizes for chapters based on the NSFH vary depending on the population being analyzed. The portion of Chapter 3 devoted to partner selection uses the NSFH. The sample size is 8,523, comprising respondents who currently are or have ever been in first marriages. Never-married respondents are omitted, as are those whose first marriages were to previously married persons. The majority of Chapter 4, examining the effects of parental divorce on offspring marital stability, analyzes the same subsample used in Chapter 3. The exception is the analysis of complete marital histories, which includes all respondents who have ever been married. Here the sample size is 8,590. Chapter 6 analyzes only the 27 percent of respondents who have ever cohabited, while excluding the approximately 3,000 respondents not re-interviewed in 1992–94. This yields a sample of 2,747.

The GSS, a national probability sample of English-speaking households within the contiguous United States, has been conducted annually or biennially since 1972.[2] Most of the items on marriage and divorce have remained consistent over time, making the GSS ideal for studying trends. I analyze the 1973–94 surveys, inclusive; the 1972 survey does not contain detailed information on respondent family structure background, while post-1994 surveys omit data on the timing of respondents' marriages. Also excluded are the African-American oversamples conducted in 1982 and 1987. The individual years of GSS data are pooled to create a single data set.

Chapter 3 uses the GSS to examine marriage timing. Both married and unmarried respondents are analyzed, yielding a sample of 23,195. This analysis excludes respondents who were in neither divorced nor intact families while growing up. Chapter 6 analyzes GSS data to study trends in marriage timing and rates of divorce transmission. Analyses of divorce transmission exclude never-married respondents, resulting in a sample of 23,274.

Survey Weights and Clustering

Both the NSFH and the GSS include survey weights. The GSS is a survey of households, within which one occupant is randomly selected to be the respondent. As a result, people from larger households are underrepresented. Corrective survey weights are available but are not used, given that preliminary analyses showed they made almost no difference. In contrast, the NSFH weights are intended to account for extensive differences between respondents. First, the weights adjust for the oversampling of minorities, newlyweds, single parents, individual parents in stepparent families, and individuals in cohabiting unions. Second, the weights account for various sources of sample selection bias. Finally, there are post-stratification adjustments in order to make the sample more closely resemble the United States population. For all of these reasons, the weights often have a substantial effect on analyses performed on the NSFH.

A common strategy for weighted data is to include the variables used to calculate the weights as independent variables in regression analyses, but this is not feasible given the complexity of the NSFH weighting scheme. On the other hand, sample weights can adversely affect standard errors, resulting in artificially inflated t-ratios.[3] I therefore report the results of significance tests based on Huber-White standard errors in order to provide more accurate t-ratios.[4] The Huber-White algorithm also adjusts for the cluster sampling employed by both the GSS and the NSFH.

The NSFH sample weights are used for all analyses in this book; the Huber-White algorithm is used for all regression analyses except the sickle model estimates of marital stability. This model is estimated using the TDA statistics program, for which the Huber-White algorithm is not implemented.[5] In these analyses the t-ratios are so large for all coefficients of interest that the weights could not have had any substantial impact on the standard errors. Moreover, unweighted models produce similar results.

Measuring Family of Origin

The GSS's relatively simple measure of parental family structure consists of two items. Respondents were first queried about household composition at the age of sixteen. If respondents were not living with both biological parents, a second item ascertained the reason. Two separate measures of family structure are created from these questions. The first asks whether a respondent's living situation at age sixteen was the product of divorce or parental separation. The second measure of family structure distinguishes respondents from divorced families by whether they are living with a stepparent. Thus each respondent falls into one of three categories: divorced single-parent family; divorced stepfamily; and nondivorced family. Although these measures are broad, they have the advantage of remaining consistent across repeated administrations of the GSS.

Models of marriage timing based on the GSS directly compare respondents from divorced families to people growing up in intact families, since change in family environment is hypothesized to produce early marriage in the children of divorce. Repeating these analyses with the family structure variables recoded to include all respondents did not substantially affect the results. All other analyses reported in this book contrast people from divorced families with all other respondents. Note that this should bias estimates of the divorce cycle downward, given that respondents from nonintact families not resulting from divorce have higher divorce rates than people from intact families (except for respondents from bereaved families).

The NSFH contains two varieties of data on family structure of origin. First, the NSFH measures up to four instances in which, while growing up, respondents stopped living with a parent, and then ascertains the reason for each such separation. Second, the NSFH contains a parent history calendar which shows what types of parent figures a respondent was living with each year, up to age nineteen. This calendar is used to detect the presence of step- or adoptive (cohabiting partners of biological parents) parents.

These two items are used to create four separate measures of family structure. On the basis of prior research, I contend that the strongest predictor of marital instability should be the number of family structure transitions experienced while growing up. This "family change" model is operationalized by combining the number of instances in which a respondent stopped living with a biological parent, stepparent, or adoptive parent due to marital disruption, with the number of additions of stepparents and adoptive parents to all families excluding those left incomplete by parental death. This yields a single index of parental relationship transitions. As over 99 percent of respondents had three or fewer transitions, I set all greater values to three.[6] This index of family structure transitions is used in Chapters 3, 4, and 6.

Given the detail of the NSFH data, information is also available on the timing of family disruptions and the duration of exposure to different types of parent figures. Neither source of information is used for two reasons.[7] First, the prior research cited here suggests that the number of family structure transitions is a better predictor than either duration or timing of how offspring will fare in their own marriages. Second, the permutations of family structures measurable by the NSFH are staggeringly complex – well over 100 combinations of parental figures are represented, and this does not even take into account data on timing, duration of exposure, or reasons for change.[8] Thus I only operationalize information from the NSFH identified as salient by prior research, instead of examining all possible dimensions of family structure. The count of family structure transitions analyzed here is similar to that used by other researchers, except for the omission of transitions resulting from parental death.[9] Research cited in Chapter 2 shows that bereaved offspring do not fare any worse in their marriages than do people from intact families. This finding was replicated with the NSFH data.

Two additional variables are constructed to test the family change model against some of the simpler measures of family structure used in past research. These include a dichotomous measure assessing whether a respondent experienced divorce or abandonment while growing up, and a measure that differentiates types of divorced families: Respondent experienced divorce or abandonment but not step- or adoptive parenting; respondent experienced divorce or abandonment and step- or adoptive parenting; and respondent experienced neither divorce nor step- or adoptive parenting. These variables, used in Chapters 3, 4, and 6, are roughly equivalent to those created from the GSS.

A fourth and final measure of family structure is used in Chapter 4 to determine how the family background of each spouse separately contributes to the divorce cycle. This item measures whether each spouse comes from a family disrupted by parental divorce or abandonment; an additional variable captures unions containing two spouses from divorced families. For this analysis, data limitations preclude the more detailed measures of family structure described above.

Socioeconomic Variables

Selected analyses involving the GSS use two socioeconomic variables. First, parental socioeconomic status (SES) is measured by education. For respondents reared in intact families and stepfamilies, I use the higher level of education between the two parents; for respondents from single-parent families I use that parent's education. This is coded as a set of dummy variables: not high school graduate; high school graduate; some college but no four-year degree; college graduate; and advanced degree. This coding scheme is used for all analyses of education based on either data set. Measures of parental income or occupational status would be useful but are not available in the GSS. An item that asks respondents to recall their families' economic well-being almost certainly fails to provide accurate information. Second, I use a set of dummy variables measuring respondent education.

For analyses based on the NSFH, three measures of parental SES are used: parental education; parental occupational prestige (Stevens-Cho scale); and a dummy variable measuring whether a respondent's family ever received public assistance. When two parents were present and employed I use the higher of their occupational prestige scores. The moderate inter-item correlation on SES variables (ranging from .01 to .45) is not a problem due to the large sample sizes.

Respondent SES in the NSFH is measured using education. Education is measured at the time respondents marry or enter cohabiting relationships, given that data quality is insufficient to code education as a time-varying covariate.

Although income data for respondents are available in both the GSS and the NSFH, I do not use them, on the grounds that changes in income may be a consequence as well as a cause of divorce. Previous research shows that respondent income cannot explain the intergenerational transmission of divorce.[10] Occupational status scores are omitted for similar reasons; for GSS respondents, they did not affect the results. A prohibitively large number of NSFH respondents – about 40 percent – are missing data on these variables.

Temporal Variables

All multivariate analyses reported in this book contain at least one of four varieties of temporal variables. The first is a measure of either birth cohort or marriage cohort (the historical period in which a marriage began). These variables account for spuriousness resulting from the increase in the divorce rate over time. Analyses of marital stability based on the NSFH, except for the analysis of entire marital histories in Chapter 4, use marriage cohort; it is not possible to also use birth cohort, because the two are almost perfectly correlated $(r = .97)$. Analyses of the stability of cohabiting unions use both birth cohort and cohabitation cohort (the historical period in which a cohabiting relationship began).

The second temporal variable, serving a more strictly methodological function, is the difference between a respondent's age at the time of the interview and the age at which that person first married. This is used in all analyses of marital stability not employing event history analytic techniques: the analysis of entire respondent marital histories (Chapter 4); and models of marital stability based on the GSS (Chapter 5). Marriage duration is a right-censored phenomenon; that is, respondents may end their marriages after they have been interviewed. Event history techniques, used in Chapters 3, 6, and elsewhere in Chapter 4, are customary for studying marital stability because they can account for the bias produced by right-censoring. The GSS lacks adequate data for event history analysis, so the difference between current age and age at first marriage is a substitute. Including this term in multivariate analyses should largely ameliorate the right-censoring bias by modeling the duration of exposure to the hazard of divorce.[11] For similar reasons AGE – AGE FIRST WED is included in analyses of entire marital histories (Chapter 4). For both the NSFH and the

GSS, AGE – AGE FIRST WED is highly correlated with birth cohort and marriage cohort, so neither of the latter two terms are used.

A third temporal variable, employed in all analyses based on the GSS (Chapters 3 and 6), is survey year. This serves three purposes. First, it accounts for period-specific changes in marriage and divorce rates occurring over the years represented by the data. Second, it accounts for year-specific survey error. Third, interacting survey year with family of origin provides a means of measuring change in the effects of parental divorce. (This will be described in greater detail.)

The fourth temporal variable is age at marriage. Used in Chapters 3, 4, and 5, marriage age is hypothesized to play an important part in explaining the relationship between parental divorce and offspring marital behavior. It is not possible to use age at union formation in Chapter 6 (examining cohabiting relationships), because it would be correlated perfectly with the other temporal variables.

One common feature of all the temporal variables is the possibility of nonlinear relationships with the different outcome variables. For example, given that marriages are particularly likely to fail in their first few years, the effect of AGE – AGE FIRST WED on marital stability should be particularly strong for low values. In order to diagnose departures from linearity, I used lowess models, which employ a moving window to calculate a local regression line for each data point.[12] The result is a nonparametric, graphical depiction of the relationship between two variables, so lowess is very useful for ascertaining functional form.

The lowess models confirmed that most of the temporal variables had nonlinear relationships with the various dependent variables. Two techniques were used to model the temporal variables correctly: logarithmic transformations; and piecewise linear splines. Logarithmic transformation refers to the natural logarithm of the temporal variable in question; this yielded predictors with an approximately linear relationship to divorce. Piecewise linear splines are constructed by dividing up continuous variables into two or more segments, each of which has a linear relationship to divorce.

Miscellaneous Variables

With one exception, identical control variables are used for the NSFH and the GSS, so they will be jointly described. Respondent Catholicism at the time of data collection is measured with a dummy variable, as is a variable indicating whether the respondent is an only child. Also included in all multivariate analyses is a variable measuring respondent gender. In addition to testing for gender differences in the divorce cycle, it is important to control for sex because men often fail to acknowledge their own divorces.[13] Race is divided into three categories (white, black, other) for both the GSS and the NSFH. Finally, select analyses based on the GSS use a variable measuring whether respondents were living in urban or rural areas at age sixteen. For this item, a city of 50,000 people, or the suburb of such a city, is considered urban.

Missing Data

The same missing data techniques are employed for both the GSS and the NSFH. When the numbers are trivial, as is the case for most variables, missing data are deleted listwise. When many data are missing, mean or median (for skewed variables) imputation is used in conjunction with a dummy variable indicating missing data. For missing data on categorical variables, an additional dummy is coded for missing data. More sophisticated missing data techniques, such as multiple imputation, do not perform appreciably better.[14]

Analysis

Chapter 3

Marriage timing is analyzed using a discrete time event history analysis, estimated via complementary log-log regression. The complementary log-log is a better estimator than logit or probit when discrete data approximate a continuous time process.[15] The discrete time model permits testing of hypotheses concerning interactions between parental divorce and duration dependence. As the GSS measures age at marriage in years, little would be gained by using a continuous time model. The hazard function is captured by a dummy variable for each year of age, up to age forty. Life tables revealed little meaningful variation in the risk of marriage beyond age forty, so for purposes of defining the hazard function, age is topcoded at forty.

Survey year is interacted with parental divorce to measure trends, reported in Chapter 6, in the marriage rate for people from divorced families. The choice of year as the temporal "index" was not consequential: A model based on birth cohort produced similar results, as did including variables for both survey year and birth cohort.

Interactions between the measures of parental divorce and each of the dummy variables measuring duration dependence are used to test age differences in marriage timing. Statistically significant interactions are retained in the final model, producing the age-specific marriage rates reported here. All interactions between family structure and duration dependence for values on the latter between age fourteen and twenty, inclusive, were statistically significant, except for that between stepparenting and marriage at age sixteen; conversely, none of the interactions between family structure and marriage after age twenty were significant. Thus the effect of parental divorce on offspring marriage timing does not vary by age for respondents remaining single past the age of twenty. Exploratory analyses revealed no three-way interactions between survey year, parental divorce, and duration dependence. Furthermore, the effects of parental divorce on offspring marital behavior did not vary by sex, race, religion, parental or offspring education, presence of siblings, or urbanicity while growing up.

Since the GSS measures parental family structure at age sixteen, there is a small chance of measurement error for respondents marrying at age fourteen or fifteen. However, most parents probably ended their marriages before the respondents' sixteenth birthdays, so these divorces would be captured by the family structure variables. Note also that the pattern of youthful marriage holds past age sixteen, when measurement error is far less likely.

The results of this analysis, reported in Figure 3.1, are presented as the results of the following equation:

$$\text{hazard ratio} = \exp(\text{FAMILY} + \text{YEARINT}^*1987.5 + \text{AGEINT}_i) \quad (1)$$

FAMILY represents the dummy variables measuring family structure background (divorced single parent or remarried divorced parent), YEARINT represents the interaction between survey year and family background, and AGEINT_i is the interaction between marrying at AGE i and coming from a divorced family. Subsequent to age twenty, AGEINT is not statistically significant and therefore drops out of Equation 1. In Chapter 3, marriage timing results for 1987–88 are reported to facilitate comparison with NSFH respondents; in Chapter 6, results are reported for various survey years. Equation 1 yields hazard ratios that represent the increased likelihood of marriage produced by parental divorce, compared to someone of the same age from an intact family.

Analyses of partner selection are conducted using logistic regression models, where the likelihood of marrying someone from a divorced family is the dependent variable. All reported results, here and elsewhere in this book, are statistically significant unless otherwise noted.

Chapter 4

Analyses of the duration of first marriages use the sickle model, a parametric event history model well suited to the study of marital stability.[16] The sickle model captures the nonmonotonic risk of divorce, which increases during the first few years of marriage and then slowly declines. This hazard function also has the attractive feature of a defective distribution: It can account for the fact that some couples never will dissolve their marriages. The sickle model assumes the following form:

$$r(t) = at(\exp[-t/b]) \quad (2)$$

where t represents marriage duration, $r(t)$ is the transition rate, and a and b are constants. Covariates are included with the a constant, while the b constant is the shape parameter:

$$b = \exp(\beta_0) \tag{3}$$

The estimated value on β_0 indicates the point in the risk function at which the odds of divorce are at their highest.

Marriage timing is measured in months. Unions ending in spousal death or intact at the time of the interview are considered censored. Couples that have been separated for a year or more are treated as divorced, given that the chance of reconciliation at this point is considered slight.[17]

The analysis of entire marital histories uses ordered probit models to predict the number of divorces reported by each respondent. The ordered probit is appropriate because the dependent variable, number of divorces, is measured ordinally. To combat right-censoring, the difference between current age and age at first marriage is included as an independent variable. About 99 percent of respondents reported fewer than four divorces, so values are topcoded at three. Note that over 100 respondents dissolved three or more marriages, so analyses based on this variable are stable. Predicted probabilities are then obtained via a regression standardization.

Alternate estimation techniques are conceivable. Poisson regression employs event counts as a dependent variable, but requires the events to be independent, an assumption that data on divorce histories violate.[18] Another possibility would be an event history analysis that treated divorce as a repeated event. However, a repeated-events model introduces the formidable problem of dependence between events. One of the most likely choices for a repeated-events model with dependent events, a fixed-effects partial likelihood model, performs poorly when the average number of events per individual is less than two.[19] This is the case here, as 74 percent of ever-married NSFH respondents have never divorced. More generally, a repeated events analysis would entail a number of untenable assumptions about the similarity of first and higher order marriages.[20]

One shortcoming of all analyses of marital stability is the inability to adjust estimates for selection into marriage. Chapters 3 and 5 show that the children of divorce now have lower marriage rates than do people raised in intact families, and it is reasonable to assume that the children of divorce who do not marry would have high divorce rates had they actually married; in other words, the same factors responsible for their low marriage rates would likely prove inimical to marital stability. For this reason, estimates of the effects of parental divorce on offspring marital stability presented in this book are probably biased downward.

Sample selection can sometimes be addressed through two-stage statistical models.[21] One difficulty is the challenge of identifying the first-stage equations. In the case of marriage and divorce, model identification requires a variable that affects the likelihood of marriage (the first stage equation) but has no logical connection to divorce (the second stage equation). Since most variables that affect one affect the other, identifying such a sample selection model is difficult.

Chapter 5

Trends in marriage timing for the children of divorce are calculated using the discrete time event history model employed in Chapter 3. I confirm the linearity of these trends by combining the GSS data into nine groups, based on survey year. For each of the nine groups the period-specific effects of parental divorce on marriage timing were calculated. Low numbers of people from divorced families, particularly from early survey years, precluded separate models for each survey year. These rates were then plotted against survey year using lowess smoothers. The result, a nonparametric depiction of trends in the effects of parental divorce, confirmed the assumption of linearity. This procedure also showed that trends in the rate of divorce transmission have been linear.

Historical changes in the intergenerational transmission of divorce are examined using logistic regression models, where the probability of divorce is the dependent variable. I measure trends in the divorce cycle by interacting survey year with the dummy variables measuring parental divorce; models using birth cohort as a temporal index produced similar results. The difference between current age and age at first marriage is included as an independent variable in order to combat right-censoring on respondents' divorce histories.

Given the presence of trends in the divorce cycle, it is possible that the hazard function of marital dissolution may itself have changed. If it changed at different rates for people from divorced and intact families, a spurious decline in the divorce cycle might be observed.[22] The children of divorce may still be dissolving their marriages with the same disproportionate frequency as in the past, but they are waiting longer to do so. This could be called time-varying right-censoring. Furthermore, if the functional form of AGE – AGE FIRST WED were not allowed to vary over historical period, the model would be misspecified and could produce erroneous results.

Preliminary analyses showed that the probability of divorce as a function of the difference between current age and age at first marriage has changed over time. Moreover, this difference has a variable effect on divorce rates for respondents from divorced and nondivorced families. On the basis of these analyses, interaction terms are included in the regressions examining trends in the divorce cycle, and their inclusion strengthens the observed decline in the rate of divorce transmission over time. However, no three-way interactions between AGE – AGE FIRST WED, historical period, and family background were identified. This suggests that time-varying right-censoring does not differ for people from divorced and intact families; thus, declines in the rate of divorce transmission cannot be attributed to the GSS's lack of proper event history data.

Trends in the divorce cycle, reported in Figures 5.3A and 5.3B, are presented as the results of the following equation:

$$\text{odds ratio} = \exp(\text{FAMILY} + \text{YEARINT} * \text{YEAR}) \qquad (4)$$

FAMILY represents the dummy variable measuring family structure background (divorced single parent or remarried divorced parent) and YEARINT represents the interaction between survey year and family background. Year is alternately set to 1973 and 1994, representing the end points of the time series, in order to capture changes over time in the rate of divorce transmission. For respondents from remarried divorced families, YEARINT is not statistically significant and therefore equals zero. Equation 4 yields survey-year-specific odds ratios that represent the increased likelihood of marital dissolution produced by parental divorce, compared to respondents who did not grow up in divorced families.

Chapter 6

I analyze cohabitation duration using Weibull parametric event history models. The Weibull specification assumes a monotonic risk function but allows the likelihood of marriage or cohabitation dissolution to increase or decrease over union duration. The assumption of monotonicity is verified by plotting $\log(-\log(G(t)))$ against $\log(t)$, where t is the survival time of cohabiting unions and $G(t)$ is the Kaplan-Meier estimate of the survivor function of t.[23] This plot depicted a straight line, confirming the appropriateness of the Weibull model.

Cohabiting relationships generally end in either marriage or dissolution, so separate models are estimated for each. Cohabiting unions ending in death are treated as censored, as are relationships intact at the time of data collection.

The hazard functions for marriage and dissolution of cohabiting relationships are different (see Figure 6.1), so analyzing them separately is statistically desirable. The likelihood functions can be separated for competing events, so it is not necessary to analyze marriage and dissolution in the same model.[24] Moreover, a competing hazards model estimated via multinomial logistic regression yielded similar results.

Evaluating the Role of Marriage Differentials in the Weakening Divorce Cycle

PROOF THAT THE RATE OF DIVORCE TRANSMISSION abated irrespective of declines in marriage for the children of divorce can be obtained from a simple standardization. To ensure adequate cases, I pooled data from the end-points of the 1973–94 General Social Survey data into two groups, representing 1973–74 and 1993–94.

For 1973–74, 28 percent (49/175) of respondents from divorced single-parent families dissolved their own marriages, compared to 17 percent (401/2388) from intact families. Marriage rates were similar for these years, with 85 percent (175/206) of people from divorced families and 88 percent (2388/2726) of people from intact families wedding. By 1994, marriage rates had declined to 68 percent (277/406) and 82 percent (2198/2676), respectively. Over the same years, divorce rates for both groups rose, to 34 percent (744/2198) for people from intact families and 42 percent (115/277) for the children of divorce; conversely, 58 percent (162/277) people from divorced families had remained married in 1994. Although divorce rates increased for both groups, their convergence demonstrates a decline in the rate of divorce transmission. At the same time, marriage rates declined much more quickly for people from divorced families than for people from intact families. Contrasting across time, 17 percent (85 – 68) fewer children of divorce married in 1993–94 than in 1973–74. Out of 406 children of divorce, 277 married in 1993–94; had marriage rates remained the same over time, 69 (.17 • 406) more would have wed.

Assume that, had they married in 1993–94, these 69 offspring from divorced families would have had the same divorce rate as other married children of divorce interviewed in these years. This is a liberal assumption: People from divorced families who were not married in the 1990s might have had higher divorce rates had they wed; in other words, the children of divorce least prepared to fare well in marriage may have been selected out of the at-risk pool for divorce. At 1993–94 levels of divorce but 1973–74 marriage rates, 29 (.42 • 69) more people would have ended a marriage than was actually the case; 40 (.58 • 69) would be married. Adding these numbers to the observed figures for 1993–94 yields 202 (162 + 40) married and 144 (115 + 29) divorced respondents from divorced families. Thus, the 1993–94 children of divorce would still have had a divorce rate of 42 percent (144/(202 + 144)) had they married at 1973–74 rates; in other words, their declining rates of marriage cannot explain the weakening divorce cycle.

The 42 percent estimate would be too low if we assume that the unmarried children of divorce in 1993–94 would have had higher divorce rates than those who did marry. Since they did not, their hypothetical divorce rate can be only speculated. Assuming a rate of 50 percent for those who would have married in 1973–74 implies that, rounding up, 35 (.5 • 69) children of divorce would have remained married and 35 (.5 • 69) would have divorced had they wed in 1993–94. Recalculating divorce rates for these years suggests that 57 percent ((162 + 35)/(277 + 69)) would have remained married and 43 percent ((115 + 35)/(277 + 69)) would have ended their own marriages.

Thus under the assumption that the hypothetical divorce rate for people from divorced families who did not marry in 1993–94 was about 20 percent (50 percent vs. 42 percent) higher than the observed rate, the overall divorce rate for the children of divorce in these years would only be 1 percent higher than the observed rate (43–42 percent) and a decline in the rate of divorce transmission would still be evident.

The effect of increased selection out of marriage over time by the children of divorce was also examined in a multivariate context, via a bivariate probit model with sample selection. The likelihood of divorce was treated as the primary dependent variable; the likelihood of marriage was the dependent variable in the selection equation, which predicted inclusion into the primary equation. This model showed that the divorce cycle weakened over time irrespective of decreased selection into marriage by the children of divorce. However, stage one of this model, marriage, was identified only via functional form and not substantive variables (see the discussion of selection model identification in Appendix A), so its results should be viewed as tentative.

Notes

One. Introduction

1. Cherlin (1992) chronicles trends in the marriage rate. For current levels, Kreider and Fields (2001). Demographers predict that the marriage rate will remain at almost 90 percent (Goldstein and Kenney 2001).
2. Cherlin (1990).
3. Cherlin (1992).
4. For current divorce rates, Bramlett and Mosher (2001); Kreider and Fields (2001); Raley and Bumpass (2003). For numbers of children projected to grow up in divorced families, Bumpass (1984). For historical changes in numbers of two-parent families, Bumpass and Sweet (1989a). For historical trends in divorce, Cherlin (1992).
5. Heaton (2002); for a contrary view, Goldstein (1999).
6. Phillips (1991); also, Cherlin (1992); Thornton (1989); Thornton and Young-DeMarco (2001).
7. On changing treatments of divorce in literature, Freeman (2003).
8. Terman (1938): 202–7.
9. Studies in the United States include: Amato (1996); Amato and Booth (1991a, 1997); Amato and DeBoer (2001); Amato and Rogers (1997); Bramlett and Mosher (2002); Bumpass, Martin, and Sweet (1991); Bumpass and Sweet (1972); Feng, Giarrusso, Bengtson, and Frye (1999); Glenn and Kramer (1987); Goldscheider and Waite (1991); Greenberg and Nay (1982); Heiss (1972); Hetherington and Kelly (2002); Jockin, McGue, and Lykken (1996); Keith and Finlay (1988); Kulka and Weingarten (1979); Kunz (2000); McGue and Lykken (1992); McLanahan and Bumpass (1988); McLeod (1991); Mueller and Pope (1977); Mueller and Cooper (1986); Pope and Mueller (1976); Powell and Downey (1997); Teachman (2002a & b); Tucker et al. (1997); Wallerstein, Lewis, and Blakeslee (2000); Wolfinger (1999, 2000, 2003a); Wolfinger, Kowaleski-Jones, and Smith (2004). Many other studies have considered individual aspects of the divorce cycle.
10. As I will show in Chapter 3, prior research has reported numerous contradictory findings on this point. Some studies show that parental divorce

leads to early wedlock, while others find the opposite (see Note 7, Chapter 3). My results reconcile these earlier findings.

11. *Inter al.*, Glenn and Kramer (1985); Webster, Orbuch, and House (1995).

12. For example, Paul (2002).

13. Amato, Loomis, and Booth (1995); Booth and Amato (2001); Jekielek (1998).

14. See, for example, Silverstein and Auerbach (1999); Stephenson (1991).

15. For a recent review of the literature, Amato (2000). Detailed accounts are provided by, *inter al.*, Hetherington and Kelly (2002); Stewart et al. (1997).

16. Dalaker (2001). On the economic consequences of divorce, Holden and Smock (1991). More recent research shows that the economic consequences of divorce, while still substantial, have declined significantly in recent years (McKeever and Wolfinger 2001). See Chapter 7 for further discussion of this issue.

17. For a review, McLoyd (1998). Also useful is the edited volume by Duncan and Brooks-Gunn (1997).

18. Waite and Gallagher (2000): 212.

19. As would be expected, the effects of divorce on offspring have inspired a voluminous literature. Two useful reviews: Amato (2000); Hetherington, Bridges, and Insabella (1998).

20. On the link between parental divorce and mortality, Friedman et al. (1995); Schwartz et al. (1995); Tucker et al. (1997).

21. On the relative importance of family structure as a predictor of offspring well-being, Cherlin (1999); Wolfinger, Kowaleski-Jones, and Smith (2004).

22. This is true even though couples who split up have had less time to produce children than do those remaining married. Sixty-one percent of newly divorced women live with children; two-thirds of these have two or more children (McKeever and Wolfinger 2001).

23. For overviews of the divorce law controversy, Nock, Wright, and Sanchez (1999); Thompson and Wyatt (1999). On the failure of covenant marriage laws in Louisiana, *New York Times* (2000a); Sanchez et al. (2001).

24. Press release issued by Georgia State Rep. Brian Joyce (R) on January 11, 1995 (http://www.mcwebs.com/bjoyce/pro111195.htm).

25. Bramlett and Mosher (2001); Kreider and Fields (2001).

26. Harris (1995, 1998).

27. Wallerstein and Blakeslee (1989); Wallerstein and Kelly (1980); Wallerstein, et al. (2000).

28. Kirn (2000).

29. Cherlin (1999): 423. For other evaluations of Wallerstein, Amato (2003); Cherlin (2000); Pollitt (2000).

Two. Why Divorce Begets Divorce

1. Cherlin (1996): 431.
2. Bumpass and Sweet (1989a).
3. It is indeed curious that this view persists, as an exhaustive literature review conducted in the early 1970s cast doubt on the father absence argument (Herzog and Sudia 1973).
4. Tessman (1978).
5. Diekmann and Engelhardt (1999); Glenn and Kramer (1987); McLanahan and Bumpass (1988); McLeod (1991); Wolfinger (2000).
6. For reviews, Amato (1994); Cherlin and Furstenberg (1994); Coleman, Ganong, and Fine (2000); Furstenberg and Cherlin (1991).
7. On problematic dynamics in stepfamilies, Hetherington and Clingempeel (1992). For a comparison of parenting practices in biological and step-families, Mason, Jay, Messick-Svare, and Wolfinger (2002).
8. Furstenberg, Morgan, and Allison (1987). Furstenberg and Cherlin (1991: 73) later qualified this finding. See also King (1994); Menning (2002); Stewart (2003).
9. Kalter, Kloner, Schreier, and Okla (1989); McLanahan (1985); Wu (1996); Wu and Martinson (1993).
10. Amato (1993); Amato and Keith (1991a & b); Herzog and Sudia (1973).
11. For example, Blankenhorn (1995); Popenoe (1996).
12. Moynihan (1965): 30.
13. McLanahan and Sandefur (1994): 7–8.
14. One example: A wave of public concern over rising divorce rates occurred at the beginning of the twentieth century (May 1980; O'Neill 1967).
15. For evidence that Moynihan's arguments predated the publication of his report, Wilson (1987): 20–1.
16. Ruggles (1994).
17. For example, Rainwater and Yancey (1967).
18. Since the early 1970s, wage polarization increased at a striking rate (*inter al.*, Karoly 1993).
19. Veroff, Douvan, and Kulka (1981).
20. For example, Stacey (1998); Thorne and Yalom (1992).
21. In sociology and other social sciences the notion of *labeling* became increasingly popular in the 1960s. Considerable evidence shows that an imputed identity may influence behavior, both by and towards the bearer of the label. For a statement of labeling theory, Becker (1963).
22. See, especially, McLanahan and Sandefur (1994).
23. For recent reviews, Amato (1999, 2000).
24. For example, Vaughan (1986).
25. Waite and Lillard (1991).
26. Chase-Lansdale, Lindsay, Cherlin, and Kiernan (1995); Cherlin, Chase-Lansdale, and McRae (1998); Cherlin et al. (1991); Cherlin, Kiernan, and

Chase-Lansdale (1995); Furstenberg and Teitler (1994); Kiernan and Cherlin (1999).

27. Kiernan and Cherlin (1999).
28. McLanahan (1983).
29. Tucker, Marx, and Long (1998) is especially useful; also, Hagan, MacMillan, and Wheaton (1996); Wood et al. (1993).
30. McLanahan, Astone, and Marks (1991).
31. It is no surprise that poor neighborhoods take their toll on children's well-being (e.g., Duncan, Brooks-Gunn, and Klebanov 1994; Sucoff and Upchurch 1998).
32. Harris (1995, 1998). For evidence of the formidable public interest in Harris's research, see the cover story in the September 7, 1998 issue of *Newsweek* ("The Parent Trap," 53–9) and a somewhat longer piece in the August 17, 1998 *The New Yorker* ("Do Parents Matter?" 54–64).
33. On the importance of peers to children's well-being, Corsaro and Eder (1995).
34. Multiple stressful events take a cumulative toll on children's well being (Rutter 1983).
35. McLanahan and Sandefur (1994): 131–132; also Tucker, Marx, and Long (1998).
36. Wallerstein and Kelly (1980).
37. Hagan, MacMillan, and Wheaton (1996).
38. Holden and Smock (1991). Note also that the economic consequences of divorce have sometimes been overstated (Braver 1999); also, the exchange between Lenore Weitzman and Richard Peterson in the June 1996 issue of *American Sociological Review*.
39. Garfinkel and McLanahan (1986); for recent figures, Dalaker (2001).
40. McKeever and Wolfinger (2001).
41. Duncan and Brooks-Gunn (1997); McLoyd (1998).
42. Conger, Conger, and Elder (1997). For an alternate view, Hanson, McLanahan, and Thomson (1997).
43. McLanahan et al. (1991). Relatedly, single mothers in 1990 were over twice as likely as two-parent families to rent rather than own their homes (United States Bureau of the Census 1994).
44. McLanahan and Sandefur (1994). More recently it has been suggested that economic factors account for an even larger portion of the relationship between parental divorce and high school graduation (Biblarz and Raftery 1999).
45. Amato and Booth (1997). These authors do show that parental income affects offspring marital quality, but this effect is largely mediated by offspring socioeconomic attainment.
46. Elder (1999).
47. On high divorce rates for the offspring of remarried families, Wolfinger (2000). On the relative incomes of step- and intact families, Bachrach

(1983); Mason and Mauldon (1996); McLanahan and Sandefur (1994); Morrison and Ritualo (2000).

48. Mueller and Pope (1977); Wolfinger (1999, 2000).
49. Axinn and Thornton (1992).
50. Pong (1997, 1998).
51. Bankston and Caldas (1998).
52. On marriage between classmates, Mare (1991).
53. *Inter al.*, Avery, Goldscheider, and Speare (1992); Axinn and Thornton (1992).
54. On the effects of parental divorce on offspring educational attainment, *inter al.*, McLanahan and Sandefur (1994); Sandefur and Wells (1999). On the relationship between education and divorce risk, Bramlett and Mosher (2002); Bumpass, Martin, and Sweet (1991); Martin and Bumpass (1989).
55. McLanahan and Bumpass (1988); Mueller and Pope (1977).
56. Glenn and Kramer (1987).
57. Jockin, McGue, and Lykken (1996); McGue and Lykken (1992); also Kendler et al. (1992).
58. Kiernan and Cherlin (1999).
59. Emery (1982); see also Emery (1988).
60. Amato (1993); Amato and Keith (1991a,b).
61. Amato and Booth (1991a); Hanson (1993); Mechanic and Hansell (1989).
62. Hess and Camera (1979); Hetherington, Cox, and Cox (1982).
63. Amato and Booth (1997); Amato et al. (1995); Booth and Amato (2001); Jekielek (1998).
64. Amato and Booth (1991a, 1997).
65. Amato and DeBoer (2001).
66. Amato and Booth (1991b); Axinn and Thornton (1996). For a qualitative treatment of the relationship between parental divorce and attitudes towards marriage, Staal (2000).
67. Amato (1996). Another study found no relationship between pro-divorce attitudes and marital dissolution (Thornton 1985).
68. Amato et al. (1995); Booth and Amato (2001); Jekielek (1998).
69. McLanahan (1988); McLanahan and Bumpass (1988).
70. For evidence that the divorce cycle does not vary by offspring gender, Wolfinger (2000). This topic is addressed in greater detail in Chapter 4. On low rates of paternal custody, Cancian and Meyer (1998).
71. McKeever and Wolfinger (in press).
72. Amato and DeBoer (2001).
73. Webster et al. (1995).
74. Glenn and Kramer (1987).
75. Wolfinger (2000).
76. For reviews, Amato (1994); Cherlin and Furstenberg (1994); Coleman et al. (2000); Furstenberg and Cherlin (1991).
77. Amato (1996); Amato and Rogers (1997); Silvestri (1992); Webster et al. (1995).

78. Amato (1996).
79. Webster et al. (1995).
80. Silvestri (1992).
81. Amato and Booth (1997, 2001); Caspi and Elder (1988).
82. Amato and Booth (1991b); Axinn and Thornton (1996).
83. Webster et al. (1995).
84. Staal (2000); Wallerstein et al. (2000).
85. Amato and Booth (1991a, 1997).
86. For example, Bramlett and Mosher (2002); Bumpass, Martin, and Sweet (1991); Martin and Bumpass (1989).
87. Scott South (1995) ruled out the alternative explanation. By taking marriage market conditions into account, he showed that hasty mate selection could not explain the relationship between youthful marriage and divorce.
88. Amato (1996); Glenn and Kramer (1987); Wolfinger (2003a).

Three. Coupling and Uncoupling

1. Goldstein and Kenney (2001).
2. Glenn (1997a).
3. Waite (1995); Waite and Gallagher (2000).
4. Amato (1988, 1991); Amato and Booth (1991a); Amato and Sobolewski (2001); Cherlin et al. (1998); McLeod (1991); Ross and Mirowsky (1999).
5. This figure is based on the marriage timing of respondents analyzed in this study, who married at earlier ages than do young people today. Furthermore, this figure presents combined data for men and women. Although women generally marry somewhat earlier than men, the overall pattern is the same for both sexes.
6. United States Bureau of the Census, Personal Communication, May 29, 2003.
7. Fields and Casper (2001).
8. Studies showing that nonintact parenting leads to early wedlock include: Aquilino (1994); Axinn and Thornton (1992, 1993); Carlson (1979); Glenn and Kramer (1987); Goldscheider and Goldscheider (1998); Keith and Finlay (1988); Kiernan (1992); McLeod (1991); Michael and Tuma (1985); Mueller and Pope (1977); Ross and Mirowsky (1999); Teachman (2004); Thornton (1991); Waite and Spitze (1981). Studies showing that divorce delays or deters marriage: Avery et al. (1992); Goldscheider and Waite (1986, 1991); Kobrin and Waite (1984); Li and Wojtkiewicz (1994); National Marriage Project (2004); South (2001). Studies finding no relationship between family structure of origin and marriage timing include: Amato and Booth (1997); Cherlin, Kiernan, and Chase-Lansdale (1995); McLanahan and Sandefur (1994); Musick and Bumpass (1998). Another study found higher rates of marriage for people from stepfamilies and lower rates for those from single-parent families

(Goldscheider and Goldscheider 1993); a more recent study showed even greater variation by family type (Teachman 2003). For reviews, Li and Wojtkiewicz (1994); Wolfinger (2003b).

9. Studies failing to distinguish between parental divorce and death include Michael and Tuma (1985); South (2001); Waite and Spitze (1981). See Chapter 2 for evidence that death has fewer consequences for offspring marital behavior than does divorce.

10. For example, Avery et al. (1992); Axinn and Thornton (1992, 1993); Goldscheider and Goldscheider (1993); Michael and Tuma (1985); Thornton (1991).

11. On the relationship between parental divorce and problematic interpersonal behaviors prior to marriage, Jacquet and Surra (2001).

12. Amato and Booth (1997); Axinn and Thornton (1993); Cherlin, Kiernan, and Chase-Lansdale (1995); Teachman (2003); Thornton (1991); also Bumpass and Sweet (1989b); Kiernan (1992).

13. Hetherington and Clingempeel (1992).

14. Goldscheider and Goldscheider (1993, 1998); Li and Wojtkiewicz (1994); Michael and Tuma (1985); Teachman (2003); Thornton (1991).

15. Holden and Smock (1991). This issue is discussed in greater detail in Chapter 7.

16. For example, Axinn and Thornton (1992); Waite and Spitze (1981).

17. Sex: Albrecht and Teachman (2003); Hogan, Sun, and Cornwell (1998); Moore and Chase-Lansdale (2001); Thornton and Camburn (1987); Wu, Cherlin, and Bumpass (1987). Pregnancy: Moore and Chase-Lansdale (2001); Wu (1996); Wu and Martinson (1993). Parental divorce also increases dating among college students (Booth, Brinkerhoff, and White 1984).

18. Hetherington (1993).

19. For a more detailed critique of earlier studies on the relationship between parental divorce and offspring marriage timing, Wolfinger (2003b).

20. All results, here and elsewhere in this book, are statistically significant unless otherwise indicated.

21. Chapter 5 shows that the relationship between parental divorce and getting married has changed substantially over time. The figures presented here are for 1987–88, the years the NSFH was initially administered, in order to facilitate comparison with the results on marital stability presented in the next chapter.

22. Goldscheider and Goldscheider (1993, 1998); Li and Wojtkiewicz (1994); Michael and Tuma (1985); Thornton (1991).

23. Axinn and Thornton (1992).

24. Axinn and Thornton (1996).

25. The early research includes Landis (1956), Mueller and Pope (1977).

26. For a recent review, Kalmijn (1998).

27. Analyzing a nonrandom sample of college students, Landis (1956) found no evidence of family structure homogamy.

28. The material in these paragraphs is derived from the detailed clinical accounts of Judith Wallerstein: Wallerstein and Blakeslee (1989); Wallerstein and Kelly (1980); conversations with Wallerstein and Glen H. Elder, Jr.; and open-ended interviews.
29. Axinn and Thornton (1996); Amato and Booth (1991a).
30. Deleire and Kalil (2002); McLanahan and Sandefur (1994).
31. Teachman (2004).

Four. How Strong Is the Divorce Cycle?

1. This refers to the first studies to employ representative data sets and multivariate analysis: Bumpass and Sweet (1972); Heiss (1972). However, earlier studies of the divorce cycle exist. See, for example, Landis (1956); Terman (1938).
2. A notable exception is Webster et al. (1995).
3. McLanahan and Bumpass (1988). This is a heavily cited paper in numerous areas of scholarship according to a review essay published in the *American Journal of Sociology* (Clemens, Powell, McIlwaine, and Okamoto 1995).
4. Mueller and Pope (1977).
5. Amato (1996).
6. Bumpass, Martin, and Sweet (1991).
7. Amato (1996); Amato and Rogers (1997); Wolfinger (2003a).
8. For example, Allison (1995).
9. Amato (1996).
10. Amato (1996); Feng et al. (1999); Glenn and Kramer (1987); Hetherington and Kelly (2002); McLeod (1991).
11. On male misrepresentation of marital histories, Bumpass, Martin, and Sweet (1991).
12. For example, Strazdins and Broom (2004); Thompson and Walker (1989).
13. On levels of remarriage, Kreider and Fields (2001). Rates of remarriage have declined in recent years, probably because people increasingly cohabit instead (Martinson 1994). On divorce rates in second marriages, Martin and Bumpass (1989).
14. Studies examining the effects of multiple family structure transitions on children includes Amato and Booth (1991a); Capaldi and Patterson (1991); Furstenberg and Seltzer (1986); Teachman (2002a); Wolfinger (2000, 2001); Wu (1996); Wu and Martinson (1993). Amato and Booth (1991a), Wolfinger (2000), and Teachman (2002a) are the only studies to consider the effect of multiple parental divorces on offspring marital stability.
15. For convenience, the terms "intact" and "nondivorced" are used interchangeably except where noted.
16. Bumpass (1984). This figure is a projection calculated for children born in the late 1970s; it provides a reasonable estimate of children's experiences with parental divorce.

17. The NSFH does not contain adequate longitudinal data, while the General Social Survey omits detailed information on respondent family background. Other data sets suffer from similar shortcomings.
18. The 1991 meta-analysis is Amato and Keith (1991a). The update is Amato (2001).
19. On family size and relative divorce risk, Waite and Lillard (1991). On the effect of siblings on rates of divorce transmission, Diekmann and Engelhardt (1999); Mueller and Pope (1977). These two studies offer contrasting results: One found that siblings increase the chances of divorce, while the other reported the opposite. Perhaps this difference can be attributed to cultural variation (one study was conducted in Germany) or the twenty-two years separating the studies.
20. On education and divorce rates, Bramlett and Mosher (2002); Bumpass, Martin, and Sweet (1991); Martin and Bumpass (1989).
21. Martin and Bumpass (1989).
22. On city size and divorce rates, Bramlett and Mosher (2002); Sweezy and Tiefenthaler (1996).
23. Amato (1996); Glenn and Kramer (1987); Wolfinger (2003a).
24. Rawlings and Saluter (1994). This refers to children in *divorced* single-mother families and excludes children living with separated single mothers.
25. Two studies (Bumpass, Martin, and Sweet 1991; McLanahan and Bumpass 1988) found no relationship between out-of-wedlock birth and marital stability, but a third showed that children born out of wedlock had higher divorce rates than offspring born to intact families (Teachman 2002a). All three studies analyzed only women, so it is not known how out-of-wedlock birth affects the marital prospects of adult male offspring.
26. Bumpass and Lu (2000).
27. Premarital childbirth and divorce: Upchurch, Lillard, and Panis (2001). Premarital cohabitation and divorce: *inter al.*, Lillard, Brien, and Waite (1995).
28. Bumpass and Lu (2000); Bumpass and Sweet (1989b).
29. Cohabitation: Brown (2002); out-of-wedlock birth: McLanahan and Sandefur (1994).
30. Upchurch et al. (2001). The relationship between premarital fertility and divorce can be explained by selection: Women predisposed to have children out of wedlock are also predisposed to have marital difficulties. Premarital fertility in itself cannot account for the high divorce rates among unmarried mothers who subsequently wed.
31. Freud (1995).
32. Erikson (1964); Tyson and Tyson (1990).
33. For a review, Hetherington, Bridges, and Insabella (1998). On the relationship between parental divorce timing and offspring marital stability, Kiernan and Cherlin (1999).
34. Freud (1965).

35. Stewart et al. (1997).
36. Powell and Downey (1997).
37. Others have argued, albeit not in the context of the divorce cycle, that some people are intrinsically prone to multiple divorces (Martin and Bumpass 1989).
38. The "starter marriage" idea has been most fully developed by Pamela Paul (2002).
39. White and Booth (1985).
40. Parental divorce has no effect on fertility within marriage (Cherlin et al. 1995).

Five. Historical Developments

1. For further discussion, Cherlin (1992).
2. Prior to 1920, divorce rates are only available as the number of divorces per thousand marriages; neither the Bureau of the Census nor the National Center for Health Statistics offers rates as the annual number of divorces per thousand married women aged fifteen and over subsequent to 1996.
3. Goldstein (1999); Kreider and Fields (2001).
4. Bramlett and Mosher (2001); Kreider and Fields (2001); Raley and Bumpass (2003).
5. Bumpass (1984). This is a projected figure.
6. Bumpass and Sweet (1989a).
7. The 1945 figure is from *Public Opinion Quarterly* (1945). The 1974 and 1998 figures were produced from the General Social Survey. See also Cherlin (1992); Thornton (1985, 1989); Thornton and Young-DeMarco (2001).
8. Phillips (1991).
9. Additional evidence for this point comes from a panel study of Detroit-area mothers and their children. From 1962 to 1993 respondents increasingly viewed divorce as an acceptable solution to a troubled marriage (Thornton and Young-DeMarco 2001).
10. Morgan (1985): 208.
11. Campbell et al. (1968): 51.
12. Wernick (1996): 64.
13. Cited in May (1980): 1.
14. For historical overviews of divorce, Blake (1962); May (1980); Phillips (1988, 1991).
15. On low conflict in modern divorces, Amato and Booth (1997).
16. Amato and Keith (1991a). A more recent meta-analysis found that effect sizes declined in the 1980s but increased again in the 1990s (Amato 2001). See Chapter 4 for a discussion of the implications of this study.
17. Li and Wojtkiewicz (1994).
18. Kulka and Weingarten (1979).
19. Goldscheider and Goldscheider (1993).

20. Bumpass, Sweet, and Cherlin (1991).
21. Fields and Casper (2001).
22. As shown in Chapter 3, teenagers from stepfamilies are even more likely to marry than are those from single-parent families. Over time, marriage rates for all children of divorce have declined at similar rates, so for simplicity I present one combined set of figures for both groups.
23. Fields and Casper (2001).
24. Wolfinger (1999).
25. Amato and DeBoer (2001).
26. Glenn and Kramer (1987). More recently, Glenn has turned this argument on its head in an attempt to explain the declining rate of divorce transmission (Glenn and Blankenhorn 1999); this piece is discussed at length in Chapter 7.
27. Goffman (1963).
28. Analyzing data from the National Surveys of Family Growth, Teachman (2002b) found that rates of divorce transmission remained stable over approximately the same years as the General Social Survey data analyzed here. Perhaps this result can be explained by the fact that his study combined respondents from divorced single- and step-parent families. Teachman also analyzed only women, whereas my study includes both sexes.

Six. The Cohabitation Revolution

1. On increases in cohabitation, Bumpass and Lu (2000); Bumpass and Sweet (1989b); Casper and Cohen (2000); Raley (2000); on declining stigma towards cohabitation, Thornton (1989); Thornton and Young-DeMarco (2001).
2. Bumpass and Lu (2000); Bumpass, Sweet, and Cherlin (1991). Moreover, rates of cohabiting parentage have increased greatly, suggesting that cohabitation is assuming more of the functions of marriage (Bumpass and Lu (2000; Bumpass and Raley 1995; Timberlake and Heuveline 2002).
3. Amato and Booth (1997); Axinn and Thornton (1993); Cherlin et al. (1995); Furstenberg and Kiernan (2001); Thornton (1991); Teachman (2003); see also Bumpass and Sweet (1989b); Kiernan (1992).
4. Furstenberg and Kiernan (2001); Kiernan and Cherlin (1999).
5. Amato and Booth (1997).
6. Axinn and Thornton (1996).
7. Bumpass and Lu (2000); Bumpass and Sweet (1989b); Casper and Cohen (2000).
8. Thornton (1991).
9. Bumpass and Sweet (1989b); Casper and Cohen (2000).
10. Bumpass and Sweet (1989b).
11. On the relative youth of cohabitors, Bumpass and Sweet (1989b); Casper and Cohen (2000).
12. On cohabitors' marriage plans, Brown and Booth (1996); also Bumpass et al. (1991).

13. Diekmann and Mitter (1984); Goldstein (1999).
14. A recent study found lower levels of commitment in cohabiting couples than in their marital counterparts (Stanley, Whitton, and Markman 2004). The small extant literature on relationship quality tells a similar story: Cohabiting partners generally report lower relationship quality than do married partners (Brown 2003; Brown and Booth 1996; Nock 1995); also see Blumstein and Schwartz (1983); Waite and Gallagher (2000). However, these studies suffer from attrition biases. Since cohabiting unions usually end so quickly, one way or another, the pool of cohabiting couples at any given point is underrepresented in people who "just left," either for marriage or dissolution.
15. On the relationship between parental divorce and problematic interpersonal behaviors prior to marriage, Jacquet and Surra (2001).
16. Axinn and Thornton (1996).
17. On the connection between parental divorce and interpersonal skills, Amato (1996); Amato and Rogers (1997); Silvestri (1992); Webster et al. (1995).
18. Ruf and Qian (1999); also Brines and Joyner (1999). For contrary findings, Bramlett and Mosher (2002).
19. Bumpass and Lu (2000).

Seven. Conclusion

1. On modern attitudes towards divorce, Kirn (1997); Thornton (1989); Thornton and Young-DeMarco (2001).
2. On the relationship of demographic attributes to divorce risk, *inter al.*, Bramlett and Mosher (2002); Heaton (2002); Raley and Bumpass (2003).
3. On rates of parental divorce, Bumpass (1984).
4. Estimate based on NSFH data; see also Martin and Bumpass (1989).
5. Teachman and Polonko (1988).
6. Bumpass (1984).
7. Amato (1996); Amato and DeBoer (2001).
8. Brown and Booth (1996); Nock (1995); Waite and Gallagher (2000).
9. Existing research on the stability of homosexual unions (e.g., Blumstein and Schwartz 1983; Kurdek 1998) does not consider any analog of the divorce cycle.
10. England: Furstenberg and Kiernan (2001); Kiernan and Cherlin (1999); Kuh and Maclean (1990). France: Traag, Dronkers, and Vallet (2000). Germany: Diekmann and Engelhardt (1999). The Netherlands: Dronkers (1997).
11. For a critique of no-fault divorce, Parkman (2000). For evidence that no-fault laws did not raise divorce rates, Glenn (1997b); Peters (1986); Schoen, Greenblatt, and Mielke (1975).
12. Blake (1962); Phillips (1991).
13. Allen (1880), cited in Blake (1962), 131.

14. May (1980).
15. O'Neill (1967).
16. This is certainly true, but many of the works cited in defense of these points have overstated their claims due to sampling issues. For years, an assertion that divorced women's standard of living declined 73 percent was the estimate most often cited by policy makers and others (Weitzman 1985). It was not shown to be in error for more than ten years (Peterson 1996). Similarly, Judith Wallerstein's often-criticized research has frequently been cited to demonstrate that divorce has adverse effects on children (Wallerstein and Blakeslee 1989; Wallerstein and Kelly 1980; Wallerstein, et al. 2000). Critiques of Wallerstein's work are surveyed in the first chapter of this book.
17. *The News Hour with Jim Lehrer*, August 20, 1997.
18. Gardiner et al. (2002). For evidence that the research of Wallerstein and Weitzman motivated proponents of divorce reform, Spaht (1998).
19. *New York Times* (2000b).
20. For Louisiana: H.B. 756 (1997); for Arizona: S.B. 1133 (1998); for Arkansas: H.B. 2039 (2001). For discussions of the passage of the Louisiana bill and the divorce reform movement in general, Nock, Wright, and Sanchez (1999); Thompson and Wyatt (1999). For a review of recent state-level legislation affecting divorce law, Gardiner et al. (2002).
21. The minuscule number of covenant marriages is attributable partially to low levels of awareness among Louisiana citizens, not to mention lack of understanding and enthusiasm by civil servants processing marriage applications (Sanchez et al. 2001).
22. On divorce rates in covenant marriages, Sanchez et al. (2003); Steven L. Nock, personal communication, June 22, 2004; see also Hawkins (2000); Nock et al. (2003).
23. Evidence of the national attention received by the marriage movement appears in *USA Today* (2000).
24. http://www.marriagemovement.org; July 15, 2000.
25. Amato and Booth (1997); Ooms (2002).
26. For an overview of state-based programs to support marriage, Gardiner et al. (2002).
27. For an overview, Stanley (2001).
28. Moon and Whitehead (in press).
29. United States Bureau of the Census, personal communication, May 29, 2003.
30. Glenn and Blankenhorn (1999); also Blankenhorn (1999)
31. Spaht (1998).
32. Garfinkel and McLanahan (1986). For recent figures, Dalaker (2001).
33. United States Bureau of the Census (2001).
34. The 14 percent figure is from McKeever and Wolfinger (2001). This finding was confirmed and updated by McKeever and Wolfinger (in press); see also Braver (1999). Estimates of the economic consequences of

divorce from the 1970s and 1980s appear in Smock (1993) and Sorensen (1992).

35. McLanahan and Sandefur (1994).
36. For example, Blake (1962).
37. Bishop (1881), cited in Blake (1962), 81.
38. Goldstein and Kenney (2001).
39. *Inter al.*, Waite (1995); Waite and Gallagher (2000).
40. Bumpass and Lu (2000).
41. Amato and Booth (1997); Amato, Loomis, and Booth (1995); Booth and Amato (2001); Jekielek (1998).
42. Amato and DeBoer (2001).
43. Amato and Booth (1997).

Appendix A. Data and Methods

1. Sweet and Bumpass (1996); Sweet, Bumpass, and Call (1988).
2. Davis and Smith (1994).
3. Winship and Radbill (1994).
4. Huber (1967); White (1980) for an overview, Greene (2002).
5. On the TDA statistics package, Blossfeld and Rohwer (1995); Rohwer (1994).
6. Over 100 respondents report having experienced three or more family structure transitions while growing up, so statistical results based on this measure of family structure should be stable.
7. See Chapters 2 and 4 for additional discussion of these issues.
8. Martinson and Wu (1992).
9. Studies using the family change model include Li and Wojtkiewicz (1994); Sandefur and Wells (1999); Teachman (2002a); Wojtkiewicz (1993); Wolfinger (2000, 2001); Wu (1996); Wu and Martinson (1993).
10. Amato (1996).
11. This technique has also been used by Glenn and Kramer (1987); Wolfinger (1999, 2000); Wolfinger et al. (2004).
12. Cleveland, Grosse, and Shyu (1992).
13. Bumpass, Martin, and Sweet (1991).
14. Paul, McCaffrey, Mason, and Fox (2001).
15. Allison (1995).
16. Blossfeld and Rohwer (1995); Diekmann and Mitter (1984).
17. Bumpass, Martin, and Sweet (1991).
18. On the independence assumption for Poisson regression, Long (1997).
19. Allison (1995).
20. Yamaguchi (1991).
21. For overviews of the voluminous literature on sample selection models, Fu, Winship, and Mare (2004); Winship and Mare (1992).
22. I thank Lawrence Wu for bringing this point to my attention.
23. Wu (1990).
24. Allison (1984).

Bibliography

Albrecht, Chris and Jay D. Teachman. 2003. "Childhood Living Arrangements and the Risk of Premarital Intercourse." *Journal of Family Issues* 24:867–94.

Allen, Nathan. 1880. "Divorces in New England." *North American Review* 80:549.

Allison, Paul D. 1984. *Event History Analysis: Regression for Longitudinal Data.* Sage University Papers on Quantitative Applications in the Social Sciences, series no. 07-046. Newbury Park, CA: Sage Publications, Inc.

Allison, Paul D. 1995. *Survival Analysis Using the SAS System: A Practical Guide.* Cary, NC: SAS Institute, Inc.

Amato, Paul R. 1988. "Long-Term Implications of Parental Divorce for Adult Self-Concept." *Journal of Family Issues* 9:201–13.

Amato, Paul R. 1991. "Parental Absence During Childhood and Depression in Later Life." *The Sociological Quarterly* 32:543–56.

Amato, Paul R. 1993. "Children's Adjustment to Divorce: Theories, Hypotheses, and Empirical Support." *Journal of Marriage and the Family* 55:23–8.

Amato, Paul R. 1994. "The Implications of Research Findings on Children in Stepfamilies." Pp. 81–87 in *Stepfamilies: Who Benefits? Who Does Not?* edited by A. Booth and J. Dunn. Mahwah, NJ: Erlbaum.

Amato, Paul R. 1996. "Explaining the Intergenerational Transmission of Divorce." *Journal of Marriage and the Family* 58:628–40.

Amato, Paul R. 1999. "Children of Divorced Parents as Young Adults." Pp. 147–163 in *Coping with Divorce, Single Parenting, and Remarriage: A Risk and Resiliency Perspective*, edited by E. Mavis Hetherington. Mahwah, NJ: Erlbaum.

Amato, Paul R. 2000. "The Consequences of Divorce for Adults and Children." *Journal of Marriage and the Family* 62:1269–87.

Amato, Paul R. 2001 "Children of Divorce in the 1990s: An Update of the Amato and Keith (1991) Meta-Analysis." *Journal of Family Psychology* 15:355–70.

Amato, Paul R. 2003. "Reconciling Divergent Perspectives: Judith Wallerstein, Quantitative Family Research, and Children of Divorce." *Family Relations* 52:318–31.

Amato, Paul R. and Alan Booth. 1991a. "Consequences of Parental Divorce and Marital Unhappiness for Adult Well-Being." *Social Forces* 69:895–914.

Amato, Paul R. and Alan Booth. 1991b. "The Consequences of Divorce for Attitudes Toward Divorce and Gender Roles." *Journal of Family Issues* 12:306–22.

Amato, Paul R. and Alan Booth. 1997. *A Generation at Risk: Growing Up in an Era of Family Upheaval.* Cambridge, MA: Harvard University Press.

Amato, Paul R. and Alan Booth. 2001. "The Legacy of Parents' Marital Discord: Consequences for Children's Marital Quality." *Journal of Personality and Social Psychology* 81:627–38.

Amato, Paul R. and Danelle DeBoer. 2001. "The Transmission of Divorce Across Generations: Relationship Skills or Commitment to Marriage?" *Journal of Marriage and Family* 63:1038–51.

Amato, Paul R. and Bruce Keith. 1991a. "Parental Divorce and the Well-Being of Children: A 'Meta-Analysis.'" *Psychological Bulletin* 110:26–46.

Amato, Paul R. and Bruce Keith. 1991b. "Parental Divorce and Adult Well-Being: A Meta-Analysis." *Journal of Marriage and the Family* 53:43–58.

Amato, Paul R., Laura Spencer Loomis, and Alan Booth. 1995. "Parental Divorce, Marital Conflict, and Offspring Well-Being During Early Adulthood." *Social Forces* 73:895–915.

Amato, Paul R. and Stacy J. Rogers. 1997. "A Longitudinal Study of Marital Problems and Subsequent Divorce." *Journal of Marriage and the Family* 59:612–24.

Amato, Paul R. and Juliana M. Sobolewski. 2001. "The Effects of Divorce and Marital Discord on Adult Children's Psychological Well-Being." *American Sociological Review* 66:900–21.

Aquilino, William S. 1994. "Family Structure and Home-Leaving: A Further Specification of the Relationship." *Journal of Marriage and the Family* 53:999–1010.

Avery, Roger, Frances Goldscheider, and Alden Speare, Jr. 1992. "Feathered Nest/Gilded Cage: Parental Income and Leaving Home in the Transition to Adulthood." *Demography* 29:375–88.

Axinn, William G. and Arland Thornton. 1992. "The Influence of Parental Resources on the Timing of the Transition to Marriage." *Social Science Research* 21:261–85.

Axinn, William G. and Arland Thornton. 1993. "Mothers, Children, and Cohabitation: The Intergenerational Effects of Attitudes and Behavior." *American Sociological Review* 58:233–46.

Axinn, William G. and Arland Thornton. 1996. "The Influence of Parents' Marital Dissolutions on Children's Attitudes Toward Family Formation." *Demography* 33:66–81.

Bachrach, Christine. 1983. "Children in Families: Characteristics of Biological, Step-, and Adopted Children." *Journal of Marriage and the Family* 45:171–79.

Bankston III, Carl L. and Stephen J. Caldas. 1998. "Family Structure, Schoolmates, and Racial Inequalities in School Achievement." *Journal of Marriage and the Family* 60:715–23.

Becker, Howard S. 1963. *Outsiders.* New York: The Free Press.

Biblarz, Timothy J. and Adrian E. Raftery. 1999. "Family Structure, Educational Attainment, and Socioeconomic Success: Rethinking the 'Pathology of Matriarchy.'" *American Journal of Sociology* 105:321–65.

Bishop, Joel P. 1881. *Commentaries on the Law of Marriage and Divorce*, 6th edition. Boston: Little, Brown & Company.

Blake, Nelson M. 1962. *The Road to Reno: A History of Divorce in the United States*. New York: Macmillan.

Blankenhorn, David. 1995. *Fatherless America: Confronting Our Most Urgent Social Problem*. New York: Basic Books.

Blankenhorn, David. 1999. "Bad Signs." *Propositions*, No. 7, Fall 1999, pp. 2–3, Institute for American Values.

Blossfeld, Hans-Peter and Götz Rohwer. 1995. *Techniques of Event History Modeling: New Approaches to Causal Analysis*. Mahwah, NJ: Erlbaum.

Blumstein, Philip and Pepper Schwartz. 1983. *American Couples*. New York: William Morrow and Company.

Booth, Alan and Paul R. Amato. 2001. "Parental Predivorce Relations and Offspring Postdivorce Well-Being." *Journal of Marriage and the Family* 63:197–212.

Booth, Alan, David B. Brinkerhoff, and Lynn K. White. 1984. "The Impact of Parental Divorce on Courtship." *Journal of Marriage and the Family* 46:85–94.

Bramlett, Matthew D. and William D. Mosher. 2001. *First Marriage Dissolution, Divorce, and Remarriage: United States*. Advance Data from Vital Health Statistics; Number 323. Hyattsville, MD: National Center for Health Statistics.

Bramlett, Matthew D. and William D. Mosher. 2002. Cohabitation, Marriage, Divorce, and Remarriage in the United States. National Center for Health Statistics, Series 23, Number 22.

Braver, Sanford L. 1999. "The Gender Gap in Standard of Living After Divorce: Vanishingly Small?" *Family Law Quarterly* 33:111–34.

Brines, Julie and Kara Joyner. 1999. "The Ties That Bind: Principles of Cohesion in Cohabitation and Marriage." *American Sociological Review* 64:333–55.

Brown, Susan L. 2002. "Child Well-Being in Cohabiting Families." Pp. 173–87 in *Just Living Together: Implications of Cohabitation on Families, Children, and Social Policy*, edited by A. Booth and A. C. Crouter. Mahwah, NJ: Erlbaum.

Brown, Susan L. 2003. "Relationship Quality Dynamics of Cohabiting Unions." *Journal of Family Issues* 24:583–601.

Brown, Susan L. and Alan Booth. 1996. "Cohabitation Versus Marriage: A Comparison of Relationship Quality." *Journal of Marriage and the Family* 58:668–78.

Bumpass, Larry L. 1984. "Children and Marital Disruption: A Replication and Update." *Demography* 21:71–82.

Bumpass, Larry L. and Hsien-Hen Lu. 2000. "Trends in Cohabitation and Implications for Children's Family Contexts in the United States." *Population Studies* 54:29–41.

Bumpass, Larry L., Teresa Castro Martin, and James A. Sweet. 1991. "The Impact of Family Background and Early Marital Factors on Marital Disruption." *Journal of Family Issues* 12:22–42.

Bumpass, Larry L. and R. Kelly Raley. 1995. "Redefining Single-Parent Families: Cohabitation and Changing Family Reality." *Demography* 32:97–109.

Bumpass, Larry L. and James A. Sweet. 1972. "Differentials in Marital Instability: 1970." *American Sociological Review* 37:754–66.

Bumpass, Larry L. and James A. Sweet. 1989a. "Children's Experience in Single-Parent Families: Implications of Cohabitation and Marital Transitions." *Family Planning Perspective* 21:256–60.

Bumpass, Larry L. and James A. Sweet. 1989b. "National Estimates of Cohabitation." *Demography* 26:615–25.

Bumpass, Larry L., James A. Sweet, and Andrew J. Cherlin. 1991. "The Role of Cohabitation in Declining Rates of Marriage." *Journal of Marriage and the Family* 53:913–27.

Campbell, Angus, Philip E. Converse, Warren E. Miller, and Donald E. Stokes. 1968. *The American Voter*. New York: John Wiley & Sons, Inc.

Cancian, Marcia and Daniel R. Meyer. 1998. "Who Gets Custody?" *Demography* 35:147–57.

Capaldi, D. M. and G. R. Patterson. 1991. "Relation of Parental Transitions to Boys' Adjustment Problems: I. A Linear Hypothesis. II. Mothers at Risk for Transitions and Unskilled Parenting." *Developmental Psychology* 27:489–504.

Carlson, Elwood. 1979. "Family Background, School and Early Marriage." *Journal of Marriage and the Family* 419:341–53.

Casper, Lynne M. and Philip N. Cohen. 2000. "How Does POSSLQ Measure Up? Historical Estimates of Cohabitation." *Demography* 37:237–45.

Caspi, Avshalom and Glen H. Elder, Jr. 1988. "Emergent Family Patterns: The Intergenerational Construction of Problem Behavior and Relationships." Pp. 218–40 in *Relationships Within Families: Mutual Influences*, edited by R. A. Hinde and J. Stevenson-Hinde. Oxford: Clarendon Press.

Chase-Lansdale, P. Lindsay, Andrew J. Cherlin, and Kathleen Kiernan. 1995. "The Long-Term Effects of Parental Divorce on the Mental Health of Young Adults: A Developmental Perspective." *Child Development* 66:1614–34.

Cherlin, Andrew J. 1990. "The Strange Case of the 'Harvard-Yale Study.'" *Public Opinion Quarterly* 54: 117–24.

Cherlin, Andrew J. 1992. *Marriage, Divorce, Remarriage*, revised edition. Cambridge, MA: Harvard University Press.

Cherlin, Andrew J. 1996. *Public and Private Families: An Introduction*. New York: McGraw-Hill.

Cherlin, Andrew J. 1999. "Going to Extremes: Family Structure, Children's Well-Being, and Social Science." *Demography* 36:421–28.

Cherlin, Andrew J. 2000. "Generation Ex-." *The Nation*. December 11, 2000, pp. 62–8.

Cherlin, Andrew J., P. Lindsay Chase-Lansdale, and Christine McRae. 1998. "Effects of Parental Divorce on Mental Health Throughout the Life Course." *American Sociological Review* 63:239–49.

Cherlin, Andrew J. and Frank F. Furstenberg, Jr. 1994. "Stepfamilies in the United States: A Reconsideration." *Annual Review of Sociology* 20:259–81.

Cherlin, Andrew J., Frank F. Furstenberg, Jr., P. Lindsay Chase-Lansdale, Kathleen E. Kiernan, Philip K. Robins, Donna Ruane Morrison, and Julien O. Teitler. 1991. "Longitudinal Studies of Effects of Divorce on Children in Great Britain and the United States." *Science* 252:1386–89.

Cherlin, Andrew J., Kathleen E. Kiernan, and P. Lindsey Chase-Lansdale. 1995. "Parental Divorce in Childhood and Demographic Outcomes in Young Adulthood." *Demography* 32:299–318.

Clemens, Elisabeth S., Walter W. Powell, Kris McIlwaine, and Dina Okamoto. 1995. "Careers in Print: Books, Journals, and Scholarly Reputations" *American Journal of Sociology* 101:433–94.

Cleveland, William S., Eric Grosse, and William M. Shyu. 1992. "Local Regression Models." Pp. 309–76 in *Statistical Models in S*, edited by J. M. Chambers and T. J. Hastie. Pacific Grove, CA: Wadsworth & Brooks.

Coleman, Marilyn, Lawrence Ganong, and Mark Fine. 2000. "Reinvestigating Remarriage: Another Decade of Progress." *Journal of Marriage and the Family* 62:1288–1307.

Conger, Rand D., Katherine Jewsbury Conger, and Glen H. Elder, Jr. 1997. "Family Economic Hardship and Adolescent Adjustment: Mediating and Moderating Processes." Pp. 288–310 in *Consequences of Growing Up Poor*, edited by G. J. Duncan and J. Brooks-Gunn. New York: Russell Sage Foundation.

Corsaro, William A. and Donna Eder. 1995. "Development and Socialization of Children and Adolescents." Pp. 452–75 in *Sociological Perspectives on Social Psychology*, edited by K. S. Cook, G. A. Fine, and J. S. House. Boston: Allyn and Bacon.

Dalaker, Joseph. 2001. U.S. Bureau of the Census, Current Population Reports Series. Pp60–214, in *Poverty in the United States: 2000*. Washington, D.C.: U.S. Government Printing Office.

Davis, James A. and Tom W. Smith. 1994. *The General Social Surveys: Cumulative Codebook, 1972–1994*. Chicago: National Opinion Research Center; http://www.norc.uchicago.edu/projects/gensoc.asp.

Deleire, Thomas and Ariel Kalil. 2002. "Good Things Come in Threes: Single-Parent Multigenerational Family Structure and Adolescent Adjustment." *Demography* 39:393–413.

Diekmann, Andreas and Henriette Engelhardt. 1999. "The Social Inheritance of Divorce: Effects of Parent's Family Type in Postwar Germany." *American Sociological Review* 64:783–93.

Diekmann, Andreas and Peter Mitter. 1984. "A Comparison of the "Sickle Function" with Alternative Stochastic Models of Divorce Rates." Pp. 123–53 in *Stochastic Modelling of Social Processes*, edited by A. Diekmann and P. Mitter. Orlando, FL: Academic Press Inc.

Dronkers, Jaap. 1997. "Zoals de ouden zongen piepen de jongen: Intergenerationele overdracht van de kans op scheiding in Nederland [Following in Their Parents' Footsteps: Intergenerational Transmission of Divorce in the Netherlands]." *Mens en Maatschappij* 72:146–65; English-language version presented at the 1997 annual meeting of the European Sociological Association, Essex.

Duncan, Greg J. and Jeanne Brooks-Gunn. 1997. *Consequences of Growing Up Poor.* New York: Russell Sage Foundation.

Duncan, Greg J., Jeanne Brooks-Gunn, and Pamela Kato Klebanov. 1994. "Economic Deprivation and Early Childhood Development." *Child Development* 65:296–318.

Elder, Jr, Glen E. 1999. *Children of the Great Depression*, 25th anniversary edition. Boulder, CO: Westview Press.

Emery, Robert E. 1982. "Interparental Conflict and the Children of Discord and Divorce." *Psychological Bulletin* 92:310–30.

Emery, Robert E. 1988. *Marriage, Divorce, and Children's Adjustment.* Beverly Hills: Sage.

Erikson, Eric H. 1964. *Childhood and Society*, 2nd edition. New York: Norton.

Feng Du, Roseann Giarrusso, Vern L. Bengtson, and Nancy Frye. 1999. "Intergenerational Transmission of Marital Quality and Marital Instability." *Journal of Marriage and the Family* 61:451–63.

Fields, Jason and Lynne M. Casper. 2001. *America's Families and Living Arrangements: March 2000.* Current Population Reports, Pp. 20–537. Washington, DC: U.S. Census Bureau.

Freeman, Kimberly A. 2003. *Love American Style: Divorce and the American Novel, 1881–1976.* New York: Routledge.

Freud, Anna. 1965. *Normality and Pathology in Childhood: Assessments of Development.* New York: International Universities Press.

Freud, Sigmund. 1995. *The Basic Writings of Sigmund Freud*, translated and edited by A. A. Brill. New York: Random House.

Friedman, Howard S., Joan S. Tucker, Joseph E. Schwartz, Carol Tomlinson-Keasey, Leslie R. Martin, Deborah L. Wingard, and Michael H. Criqui. 1995. "Psychosocial and Behavioral Predictors of Longevity: The Aging and Death of the 'Termites.'" *American Psychologist* 50:69–78.

Fu, Vincent Kang, Christopher Winship, and Robert D. Mare. 2004. "Sample Selection Bias Models." *Handbook of Data Analysis*, edited by A. E. Bryman and M. A. Hardy. Thousand Oaks, CA: Sage.

Furstenberg, Jr., Frank F. and Andrew J. Cherlin. 1991. *Divided Families: What Happens to Children When Parents Part.* Cambridge, MA: Harvard University Press.

Furstenberg, Jr., Frank F. and Kathleen E. Kiernan. 2001. "Delayed Parental Divorce: How Much Do Children Benefit?" *Journal of Marriage and the Family* 63:446–457.

Furstenberg, Jr., Frank F., S. Philip Morgan, and Paul D. Allison. 1987. "Paternal Participation and Children's Well-Being after Marital Dissolution." *American Sociological Review* 52:695–701.

Furstenberg, Jr., Frank F. and Judith A. Seltzer. 1986. "Divorce and Child Development." Pp. 127–60 in *Sociological Studies of Child Development, Vol. 1*, edited by P. A. Adler and P. Adler. Greenwich, CT: JAI Press Inc.

Furstenberg, Jr., Frank F. and Julien O. Teitler. 1994. "Reconsidering the Effects of Marital Disruption: What Happens to Children of Divorce in Early Adulthood?" *Journal of Family Issues* 15:173–90.

Gardiner, Karen, Mike Fishman, Plamen Nikolov, and Stephanie Laud. 2002. "State Policies to Promote Marriage." Preliminary report submitted to the U.S. Department of Health and Human Services, Office of the Assistant Secretary for Planning and Evaluation.

Garfinkel, Irwin and Sarah S. McLanahan. 1986. *Single Mothers and Their Children: A New American Dilemma*. Washington, D.C.: The Urban Institute Press.

Glenn, Norval D. 1997a. *Closed Hearts, Closed Minds: The Textbook Story of Marriage*. New York: Institute for Family Values.

Glenn, Norval D. 1997b. "A Reconsideration of the Effect of No-Fault Divorce on Divorce Rates." *Journal of Marriage and the Family* 59:1023–25.

Glenn, Norval D. and David Blankenhorn. 1999. "Look Closely at 'Good News' on Divorce: It's Not that Fewer Children of Divorce are Divorcing. More Children of Intact Families Are." *Los Angeles Times*, November 15, 1999.

Glenn, Norval D. and Kathryn B. Kramer. 1985. "The Psychological Well-Being of Adult Children of Divorce." *Journal of Marriage and the Family* 47:905–12.

Glenn, Norval D. and Kathryn B. Kramer. 1987. "The Marriages and Divorces of the Children of Divorce." *Journal of Marriage and the Family* 49:811–25.

Goffman, Erving. 1963. *Stigma: Notes on the Management of Spoiled Identity*. Englewood Cliffs, NJ: Prentice Hall.

Goldscheider, Frances K. and Calvin Goldscheider. 1993. *Leaving Home Before Marriage: Ethnicity, Familism, and Generational Relationships*. Madison, WI: The University of Wisconsin Press, 1993.

Goldscheider, Frances K. and Calvin Goldscheider. 1998. "The Effects of Childhood Family Structure on Leaving and Returning Home." *Journal of Marriage and the Family* 60:745–56.

Goldscheider, Frances K. and Linda J. Waite. 1986. "Sex Differences in the Entry into Marriage." *American Journal of Sociology* 92:91–109.

Goldscheider, Frances K. and Linda J. Waite. 1991. *New Families, No Families? The Transformation of the American Home*. Berkeley, CA: University of California Press.

Goldstein, Joshua R. 1999. "The Leveling of Divorce in the United States." *Demography* 36:409–414.

Goldstein, Joshua R. and Catherine T. Kenney. 2001. "Marriage Delayed or Marriage Foregone? New Cohort Forecasts of First Marriage for U.S. Women." *American Sociological Review* 66:506–19.

Greenberg, Ellen F. and W. Robert Nay. 1982. "The Intergenerational Transmission of Marital Instability Reconsidered." *Journal of Marriage and the Family* 44:335–47.

Greene, William H. 2002. *Econometric Analysis*, 5th ed. Englewood Cliffs, N.J.: Prentice Hall.

Hagan, John, Ross MacMillan, and Blair Wheaton. 1996. "New Kid in Town: Social Capital and the Life Course Effects of Family Migration on Children." *American Sociological Review* 61:368–85.

Hanson, Thomas L. 1993. *Family Structure, Parental Conflict, and Child Well-Being.* Unpublished doctoral dissertation, Department of Sociology University of Wisconsin-Madison.

Hanson, Thomas L., Sara McLanahan, and Elizabeth Thomson. 1997. "Economic Resources, Parental Practices, and Children's Well-Being." Pp. 190–238 in *Consequences of Growing Up Poor*, edited by G. J. Duncan and J. Brooks-Gunn. New York: Russell Sage Foundation.

Harris, Judith Rich. 1995. "Where Is the Child's Environment? A Group Socialization Theory of Development." *Psychological Review* 102:458–89.

Harris Judith Rich. 1998. *The Nurture Assumption: Why Children Turn Out the Way They Do; Parents Matter Less Than You Think and Peers Matter More.* New York: Free Press.

Hawkins, Alan J. 2000. "How Do We Measure Our Success? Lessons from Covenant Marriage Legislation in Louisiana." Paper presented at the 2000 annual Smart Marriages/Happy Families Conference, Denver.

Heaton, Tim B. 2002. "Factors Contributing to Increasing Marital Stability in the United States." *Journal of Family Issues* 23:392–409.

Heiss, Jerold. 1972. "On the Transmission of Marital Instability in Black Families." *American Sociological Review* 37:82–92.

Herzog, Elizabeth and Cecilia E. Sudia. 1973. "Children in Fatherless Families." Pp. 141–232 in *Review of Child Development Research*, Vol. 3, edited by B. M. Caldwell and N. H. Ricciuti. Chicago: University of Chicago Press.

Hess, Robert D. and Kathleen A. Camera. 1979. "Post-Divorce Family Relations as Mediating Factors in the Consequences of Divorce for Children." *The Journal of Social Issues* 35:79–96.

Hetherington, E. Mavis. 1993. "An Overview of the Virginia Longitudinal Study of Divorce and Remarriage with a Focus on Early Adolescence." *Journal of Family Psychology* 7:39–56.

Hetherington, E. Mavis, Margaret Bridges, and Glendessa M. Insabella. 1998. "What Matters? What Does Not? Five Perspectives on the Association Between Marital Transitions and Children's Adjustment." *American Psychologist* 63:167–84.

Hetherington, E. Mavis and William G. Clingempeel. 1992. "Coping with Marital Transitions: A Family Systems Perspective." *Monographs of the Society for Research in Child Development* 57:1–242.

Hetherington, E. Mavis, Martha Cox, and Roger Cox. 1982. "Effects of Divorce on Parents and Children." Pp. 233–88 in *Nontraditional Families: Parenting and Child Development*, edited by M. Lamb. Mahwah, NJ: Erlbaum.

Hetherington, E. Mavis and John Kelly. 2002. *For Better or for Worse: Divorce Reconsidered*. New York: W.W. Norton & Company.

Hogan, Dennis P., Rongjun Sun, and Gretchen T. Cornwell. 1998. "Cohort Differences, Family Structure, and Adolescent Sexual Activity." Paper presented at the 1998 Annual Meeting of the American Sociological Association, San Francisco.

Holden, Karen C. and Pamela J. Smock. 1991. "The Economic Costs of Marital Disruption: Why Do Women Bear a Disproportionate Cost?" *Annual Review of Sociology* 17:51–78.

Huber, P. J. 1967. "The Behavior of Maximum Likelihood Estimates Under Non-Standard Conditions." *Proceedings of the Fifth Berkeley Symposium on Mathematical Statistics and Probability* 1:221–33.

Jacquet, Susan E. and Catherine A. Surra. 2001. "Parental Divorce and Premarital Couples: Commitment and Other Relationship Characteristics." *Journal of Marriage and Family* 63:627–38.

Jekielek, Susan M. 1998. "Parental Conflict, Marital Disruption, and Children's Emotional Well-Being." *Social Forces* 76:905–36.

Jockin, Victor, Matt McGue, and David T. Lykken. 1996. "Personality and Divorce: A Genetic Analysis." *Journal of Personality and Social Psychology* 71:288.

Kalmijn, Matthijs. 1998. "Intermarriage and Homogamy: Causes, Patterns, Trends." *Annual Review of Sociology* 24:395–421.299.

Kalter, Neil, Amy Kloner, Shelly Schreier, and Katherine Okla. 1989. "Predictors of Children's Postdivorce Adjustment." *American Journal of Orthopsychiatry* 59:605–18.

Karoly, Lynn. 1993. "The Trend in Inequality Among Families, Individuals, and Workers in the United States: A Twenty-Five Year Perspective." Pp. 19–97 in *Uneven Tides*, edited by S. Danziger and P. Gottschalk. New York: Russell Sage.

Keith, Verna M. and Barbara Finlay. 1988. "The Impact of Parental Divorce on Children's Educational Attainment, Marriage Timing, and Likelihood of Divorce." *Journal of Marriage and the Family* 50:797–809.

Kendler, Kenneth S., Michael C. Neale, Ronald C. Kessler, Andrew C. Heath, and J. J. Eaves. 1992. "Childhood Parental Loss and Adult Psychopathology in Women: A Twin Study Perspective." *Archives of General Psychiatry* 29:109–16.

Kiernan, Kathleen E. 1992. "The Impact of Family Disruption in Childhood on Transitions Made in Young-Adult Life." *Population Studies* 46:213–34.

Kiernan, Kathleen E. and Andrew J. Cherlin. 1999. "Parental Divorce and Partnership Dissolution in Adulthood: Evidence from a British Cohort Study." *Populations Studies* 32:39–48.

King, Valerie. 1994. "Nonresident Father Involvement and Child Well-Being: Can Dads Make a Difference?" *Journal of Family Issues* 15:78–96.

Kirn, Walter. 1997. "The Ties That Bind." *Time*, August 18, Vol. 150, No. 7, 48–50.

Kirn, Walter. 2000. "Should You Stay Together for the Kids?" *Time*, September 25, Vol. 156, No. 13, 74–80.

Kobrin, Frances E. and Linda J. Waite. 1984. "Effects of Childhood Family Structure on the Transition to Marriage." *Journal of Marriage and the Family* 46:807–16.

Kreider, Rose M. and Jason M. Fields. 2001. *Number, Timing, and Duration of Marriages and Divorces: Fall 1996.* Current Population Reports, Pp. 70–80. Washington, DC: U.S. Census Bureau.

Kuh, Diana and Mavis Maclean. 1990. "Women's Childhood Experience of Parental Separation and Their Subsequent Health and Socio-Economic Status in Adulthood." *Journal of Biosocial Science* 22:121–35.

Kulka, Richard A. and Helen Weingarten. 1979. "The Long-Term Effects of Parental Divorce in Childhood in Adult Adjustment." *The Journal of Social Issues* 35:50–78.

Kunz, Jenifer. 2000. "The Intergenerational Transmission of Divorce: A Nine Generation Study." *Journal of Divorce and Remarriage* 34:169–175.

Kurdek, Lawrence A. 1998. "Relationship Outcomes and Their Predictors: Longitudinal Evidence from Heterosexual Married, Gay Cohabiting, and Lesbian Cohabiting Couples." *Journal of Marriage and the Family* 60:553–68.

Landis, Judson T. 1956. "The Pattern of Divorce in Three Generations." *Social Forces* 34:213–16.

Li, Jiang H. and Roger A. Wojtkiewicz. 1994. "Childhood Family Structure and Entry into First Marriage." *The Sociological Quarterly* 35:247–68.

Lillard, Lee A., Michael J. Brien, and Linda J. Waite. 1995. "Premarital Cohabitation and Subsequent Marital Dissolution: A Matter of Self-Selection?" *Demography* 32:437–57.

Long, J. Scott. 1997. *Regression Models for Categorical and Limited Dependent Variables.* Thousand Oaks, CA: Sage.

Mare, Robert D. 1991. "Five Decades of Educational Assortative Mating." *American Sociological Review* 56:15–32.

Martin, Theresa Castro and Larry L. Bumpass. 1989. "Recent Trends in Marital Disruption." *Demography* 26:37–51.

Martinson, Brian C. 1994. "Postmarital Union Formation: Trends and Determinants of the Competing Roles of Remarriage and Nonmarital Cohabitation Among Women in the United States." Unpublished doctoral dissertation, Department of Sociology, University of Wisconsin-Madison.

Martinson, Brian C. and Lawrence L. Wu. 1992. "Parent Histories: Patterns of Change in Early Life." *Journal of Family Issues* 13:351–77.

Mason, Mary Ann, Sidney Jay, Gloria Messick-Svare, and Nicholas H. Wolfinger. 2002. "Stepparents: De Facto Parents or Legal Strangers?" *Journal of Family Issues* 23:507–22.

Mason, Mary Ann and Jane Mauldon. 1996. "The New Stepfamily Requires a New Public Policy." *Journal of Social Issues* 52:11–27.

May, Elaine Tyler. 1980. *Great Expectations: Marriage and Divorce in Post-Victorian America.* Chicago: University of Chicago Press.

McGue, Matt and David T. Lykken. 1992. "Genetic Influence on Risk of Divorce." *Psychological Science* 6:368–73.

McKeever, Matthew and Nicholas H. Wolfinger. 2001. "Reexamining the Economic Consequences of Marital Disruption for Women." *Social Science Quarterly* 82:202–17.

McKeever Matthew and Nicholas H. Wolfinger. In press. "Shifting Fortunes in a Changing Economy: Trends in the Economic Well-Being of Divorced Women." In *Fragile Families and the Marriage Agenda*, edited by L. Kowaleski-Jones and N. H. Wolfinger. New York: Kluwer.

McLanahan, Sara S. 1983. "Family Structure and Stress: A Longitudinal Comparison of Two-Parent and Female-Headed Families." *Journal of Marriage and the Family* 45:347–57.

McLanahan, Sara S. 1985. "Family Structure and the Reproduction of Poverty." *American Journal of Sociology* 90:873–901.

McLanahan, Sara S. 1988. "Family Structure and Dependency: Early Transitions to Female Household Headship." *Demography* 25:1–16.

McLanahan, Sara S., Nan Marie Astone, and Nadine F. Marks. 1991. "The Role of Mother-Only Families in the Reproduction of Poverty." Pp. 51–78 in *Children in Poverty*, edited by A. C. Huston. New York: Cambridge University Press.

McLanahan, Sara S. and Larry L. Bumpass. 1988. "Intergenerational Consequences of Family Disruption." *American Journal of Sociology* 94:130–52.

McLanahan, Sara S. and Gary Sandefur. 1994. *Growing Up with a Single Parent: What Hurts, What Helps.* Cambridge, MA: Harvard University Press.

McLeod, Jane D. 1991. "Childhood Parental Loss and Adult Depression." *Journal of Health and Social Behavior* 32:205–20.

McLoyd, Vonnie C. 1998. "Socioeconomic Disadvantage and Child Development." *American Psychologist* 53:185–204.

Mechanic, David and Stephen Hansell. 1989. "Divorce, Family Conflict, and Adolescents' Well-Being." *Journal of Health and Social Behavior* 30:105–16.

Menning, Chadwick L. 2002. "Absent Parents Are More Than Money: The Joint Effect of Activities and Financial Support on Children's Educational Attainment." *Journal of Family Issues* 23:648–71.

Michael, Robert and Nancy Brandon Tuma. 1985. "Entry into Marriage and Parenthood by Young Men and Women: The Influence of Family Background." *Demography* 22:515–44.

Moon, Dawne and Jaycee Whitehead. In press. "Marrying for America: A Feminist Discursive Approach to National Intimacy." In *Fragile Families and the Marriage Agenda*, edited by L. Kowaleski-Jones and N. H. Wolfinger. New York: Kluwer.

Moore, Mignon R. and P. Lindsay Chase-Lansdale. 2001. "Sexual Intercourse and Pregnancy Among African American Girls in High-Poverty Neighborhoods: The Role of Family and Perceived Community Environment." *Journal of Marriage and Family* 63:1146–57.

Morgan, Ted. 1985. *FDR: A Biography*. New York: Simon and Schuster.

Morrison, Donna Ruane and Amy Ritualo. 2000. "Routes to Children's Economic Recovery After Divorce: Are Cohabitation and Remarriage Equivalent?" *American Sociological Review* 65:560–80.

Moynihan, Daniel P. 1965. *The Negro Family: The Case for National Action*. Washington, DC: U.S. Department of Labor, Office of Policy Planning and Research.

Mueller, Charles W. and Hallowell Pope. 1977. "Marital Instability: A Study of Its Transmission Between Generations." *Journal of Marriage and the Family* 39:83–93.

Mueller, Daniel P. and Philip W. Cooper. 1986. "Children of Single Parent Families: How They Fare as Young Adults." *Family Relations* 35:169–76.

Musick, Kelly and Larry L. Bumpass. 1998. "How Do Prior Experiences in the Family Affect Transitions to Adulthood?" NSFH Working Paper No. 81, Center for Demography and Ecology, University of Wisconsin-Madison.

National Marriage Project. 2004. *The State of Our Unions: The Social Health of Marriage in America*, Rutgers University.

New York Times. 2000a. "States Declare War on Divorce Rates Before Any 'I Do's,'" April 21, 2000.

New York Times. 2000b. "The Republicans; Excerpts from Platform Approved by Republican National Convention," August 1, 2000.

Nock, Steven L. 1995. "A Comparison of Marriages and Cohabiting Relationships." *Journal of Family Issues* 16:53–76.

Nock, Steven L., Laura Sanchez, Julia C. Wilson, and James D. Wright. 2003. "Intimate Equality: The Early Years of Covenant and Standard Marriages." Paper presented at the 2003 annual meeting of the Population Association of America, Minneapolis.

Nock, Steven L., James D. Wright, and Laura Sanchez. 1999. "America's Divorce Problem." *Society* 36:43–52.

O'Neill, William L. 1967. *Divorce in the Progressive Era*. New Haven: Yale University Press.

Ooms, Theodora. 2002. "Marriage Plus." *The American Prospect*, Vol. 13, No. 7.

Parkman, Allen M. 2000. *Good Intentions Gone Awry: No-Fault Divorce and the American Family*. Lanham, MD: Rowman & Littlefield.

Paul, Christopher, Daniel McCaffrey, William M. Mason, and Sarah A. Fox. 2001. "What Should We Do About Missing Data? A Case Study Using

Logistic Regression with Data Missing on a Single Covariate." Unpublished paper, RAND.

Paul, Pamela. 2002. *The Starter Marriage and the Future of Matrimony.* New York: Villard Books.

Peters, Elizabeth H. 1986. "Marriage and Divorce: Informational Constraints and Private Contracting." *American Economic Review* 76:437–54.

Peterson, Richard R. 1996. "A Re-Evaluation of the Economic Consequences of Divorce." *American Sociological Review* 61:528–36.

Phillips, Roderick. 1988. *Putting Asunder: A History of Divorce in Western Society.* New York: Cambridge University Press.

Phillips Roderick. 1991. *Untying the Knot: A Short History of Divorce.* New York: Cambridge University Press.

Pollitt, Katha. 2000. "Social Pseudoscience." *The Nation,* October 23, 2000, P. 10.

Pope, Hallowell and Charles W. Mueller. 1976. "The Intergenerational Transmission of Marital Instability: Comparisons by Race and Sex." *The Journal of Social Issues* 32:49–66.

Popenoe, David. 1996. *Life Without Father.* New York: The Free Press.

Pong, Suet-Ling. 1997. "Family Structure, School Context, and Eighth-Grade Math and Reading Achievement." *Journal of Marriage and the Family* 59:734–46.

Pong, Suet-Ling. 1998. "The School Compositional Effect of Single Parenthood on Tenth-Grade Achievement." *Sociology of Education* 71:24–43.

Powell, Brian and Douglas B. Downey. 1997. "Living in Single-Parent Households: An Investigation of the Same-Sex Hypothesis." *American Sociological Review* 62:521–39.

Public Opinion Quarterly. 1945. "The Quarter's Polls." 9:223–57.

Rainwater, Lee and William L. Yancey. 1967. *The Moynihan Report and the Politics of Controversy.* Cambridge, MA: MIT Press.

Raley, R. Kelly. 2000. "Recent Trends and Differentials in Marriage and Cohabitation: The United States." Pp. 19–39 in *The Ties that Bind: Perspectives on Marriage and Cohabitation,* edited by L. J. Waite. New York: Aldine de Gruyter.

Raley, R. Kelly and Larry Bumpass. 2003. "The Topography of the Divorce Plateau: Levels and Trends in Union Stability in the United States after 1980." *Demographic Research* 8:245–60.

Rawlings, Steve W. and Arlene F. Saluter. 1994. *Household and Family Characteristics: March 1994,* U.S. Bureau of the Census, Current Population Reports, P.20-483. Washington, D.C.: U.S. Government Printing Office.

Rohwer, Götz. 1994. *TDA working papers.* Bremen: University of Bremen.

Ross, Catherine E. and John Mirowsky. 1999. "Parental Divorce, Life-Course Disruption, and Adult Depression." *Journal of Marriage and the Family* 61:1034–45.

Ruf, Stacey D. and Zhenchao Qian. 1999. "Stability of Cohabitation: The Impact of Socio-Demographic Characteristics." Paper presented at the 1999 annual meeting of the Population Association of America, New York.

Ruggles, Steven. 1994. "The Origins of African-American Family Structure." *American Sociological Review* 59:136–51.

Rutter, Michael. 1983. "Stress, Coping, and Development: Some Issues and Some Questions." Pp. 1–42 in *Stress, Coping, and Development in Children*, edited by N. Garmezy and M. Rutter. New York: McGraw Hill.

Sanchez, Laura, Steven L. Nock, Jill A. Deines, and James D. Wright. 2003. "Can Covenant Marriage Foster Marital Stability Among Low-Income, Fragile Newlyweds?" National Poverty Conference on Marriage and Family Formation Among Low-Income Couples: What Do We Know from Research?, Washington DC.

Sanchez, Laura, Steven L. Nock, James D. Wright, Jessica W. Pardee, and Marcel Ionescu. 2001. "The Implementation of Covenant Marriage in Louisiana." Paper presented at the 2001 annual meeting of the Population Association of America, Washington DC.

Sandefur, Gary D. and Thomas Wells. 1999. "Does Family Structure Really Influence Educational Attainment?" *Social Science Research* 28:331–57.

Schoen, Robert, Harry N. Greenblatt, and Robert B. Mielke. 1975. "California's Experience with No-Fault Divorce." *Demography* 12:223–44.

Schwartz, Joseph, Howard S. Friedman, Joan S. Tucker, Carol Tomlinson-Keasey, Deborah L. Wingard, and Michael H. Criqui. 1995. "Sociodemographic and Psychosocial Factors in Childhood as Predictors of Adult Mortality." *American Journal of Public Health* 85:1237–45.

Silverstein, Louise B. and Carl F. Auerbach. 1999. "Deconstructing the Essential Father." *American Psychologist* 54:397–407.

Silvestri, Silvio. 1992. "Marital Instability in Men from Intact and Divorced Families: Interpersonal Behavior, Cognitions, and Intimacy." *Journal of Divorce and Remarriage* 18:79–108.

Smock, Pamela J. 1993. "The Economic Costs of Marital Disruption for Young Women Over the Past Two Decades." *Demography* 30:353–71.

Sorensen, Annemette. 1992. "Estimating the Economic Consequences of Separation and Divorce: A Cautionary Tale from the United States." Pp. 262–82 in *Economic Consequences of Divorce: The International Perspective*, edited by L. J. Weitzman and M. Maclean. Oxford: Clarendon Press.

South, Scott J. 1995. "Do You Need To Shop Around? Age at Marriage, Spousal Alternatives, and Marital Dissolution." *Journal of Family Issues* 16:432–49.

South, Scott J. 2001. "The Variable Effects of Family Background on the Timing of First Marriage: United States, 1969–1993." *Social Science Research* 30:606–26.

Spaht, Katherine Shaw. 1998. "Why Covenant Marriage? A Change in Culture for the Sake of the Children." *Louisiana Bar Journal* 46:116–19.

Staal, Stephanie. 2000. *The Love They Lost: Living with the Legacy of Our Parents' Divorce*. New York: Delacorte Press.

Stacey, Judith. 1998. *Brave New Families*. Berkeley, CA: University of California Press.

Stanley, Scott M. 2001. "Making a Case for Premarital Education." *Family Relations* 50:272–80.

Stanley, Scott M., Sarah W. Whitton, and Howard J. Markman. 2004. "Maybe I Do: Interpersonal Commitment and Marital or Nonmarital Cohabitation." *Journal of Family Issues* 25:496–519.

Stephenson, June. 1991. *The Two-Parent Family Is Not the Best*. Napa, CA: Diemer, Smith.

Stewart, Abigail J., Anne P. Copeland, Nia Lane Chester, Janet E. Malley, and Nicole B. Barenbaum. 1997. *Separating Together: How Divorce Transforms Families*. New York: The Guilford Press.

Stewart, Susan D. 2003. "Nonresident Parenting and Adolescent Adjustment." *Journal of Family Issues* 24:217–44.

Strazdins, Lyndall and Dorthy H. Broom. 2004. "Acts of Love (and Work): Gender Imbalance in Emotional Work and Women's Psychological Distress." *Journal of Family Issues* 25:356–78.

Sucoff, Clea A. and Dawn M. Upchurch. 1998. "Neighborhood Context and the Risk of Childbearing Among Metropolitan-Area Black Adolescents." *American Sociological Review* 63:571–85.

Sweet, James A. and Larry L. Bumpass. 1996. "The National Survey of Families and Households – Waves 1 and 2: Data Description and Documentation." Center for Demography and Ecology, University of Wisconsin-Madison.

Sweet, James A., Larry L. Bumpass, and Vaughn R. A. Call. 1988. "The Design and Content of the National Survey of Families and Households." NSFH Working Paper No. 1, Center for Demography and Ecology, University of Wisconsin-Madison; http://www.ssc.wisc.edu/nsfh/home.htm.

Sweezy, Kate and Jill Tiefenthaler. 1996. "Do State-Level Variables Affect Divorce Rates?" *Review of Social Economy* 54:47–65.

Teachman, Jay D. 2002a. "Childhood Living Arrangements and the Intergenerational Transmission of Divorce." *Journal of Marriage and Family* 64:717–29.

Teachman, Jay D. 2002b. "Stability Across Cohorts in Divorce Risk Factors." *Demography* 39:331–51.

Teachman, Jay D. 2003. "Childhood Living Arrangements and the Formation of Coresidential Unions." *Journal of Marriage and Family* 65:507–24.

Teachman, Jay D. 2004. "The Childhood Living Arrangements of Children and the Characteristics of Their Marriages." *Journal of Family Issues* 25:86–111.

Teachman, Jay D. and Karen A. Polonko. 1988. "Marriage, Parenthood, and the College Enrollment of Men and Women." *Social Forces* 67:512–23.

Terman, Lewis M. 1938. *Psychological Factors in Marital Happiness*. New York: McGraw-Hill.

Tessman, Lora Heims. 1978. *Children of Parting Parents*. New York: J. Aronson.

Thompson, Linda and Alexis J. Walker. 1989. "Gender in Families: Women and Men in Marriage, Work, and Parenthood." *Journal of Marriage and the Family* 51:873–93.

Thompson, Ross A. and Jennifer M. Wyatt. 1999. "Values, Policy, and Research on Divorce: Seeking Fairness for Children." Pp. 191–232 in *The Postdivorce Family: Children, Parenting, and Society*, edited by R. A. Thompson and P. R. Amato. Thousand Oaks, CA: Sage.

Thorne, Barrie with Marilyn Yalom. 1992. *Rethinking the Family: Some Feminist Questions*, 2nd edition. Boston: Northeastern University Press.

Thornton, Arland. 1985. "Changing Attitudes Toward Separation and Divorce: Causes and Consequences." *American Journal of Sociology* 90:856–72.

Thornton, Arland. 1989. "Changing Attitudes Toward Family Issues in the United States." *Journal of Marriage and the Family* 51:873–93.

Thornton, Arland. 1991. "Influence of the Marital History of Parents on the Marital and Cohabitational Experiences of Children." *American Journal of Sociology* 96:868–94.

Thornton, Arland and Donald Camburn. 1987. "The Influence of the Family on Premarital Sexual Attitudes and Behavior." *Demography* 24:323–40.

Thornton, Arland and Linda Young-DeMarco. 2001. "Four Decades of Trends in Attitudes Toward Family Issues in the United States." *Journal of Marriage and Family* 63:1009–37.

Timberlake, Jeffrey M. and Patrick Heuveline. 2002. "Changes in Non-Marital Cohabitation and the Family Structure Experiences of Children." Paper presented at the 2002 annual meeting of the American Sociological Association, Chicago.

Traag, Tanja, Jaap Dronkers, and Louis-Andre Vallet. 2000 "The Intergenerational Transmission of Divorce Risks in France." Paper presented at the 2000 Conference of Research Committee 28 (Social Stratification), International Sociological Association, Libourne, France.

Tucker, C. Jack, Jonathan Marx, and Larry Long. 1998. "'Moving On': Residential Mobility and Children's School Lives." *Sociology of Education* 71:111–29.

Tucker, Joan S., Howard S. Friedman, Joseph E. Schwartz, Michael H. Criqui, Carol Tomlinson-Keasey, Deborah L. Wingard, and Leslie R. Martin. 1997. "Parental Divorce: Effects on Individual Behavior and Longevity." *Journal of Personality and Social Psychology* 73:381–91.

Tyson, Phyllis and Robert L. Tyson. 1990. *Psychoanalytic Theories of Development: An Integration*. New Haven, CT: Yale University Press.

USA Today. 2000. "The Matrimony Manifesto Coalition Takes Up Arms Against USA's 'Culture of Divorce,'" June 29, 2000.

United States Bureau of the Census. 1994. *Housing in Metropolitan Areas-Single-Parent Families*. Census Statistical Briefs SB/94–26. Washington, DC: U.S. Census Bureau.

United States Bureau of the Census. 2001 *Statistical Abstract of the United States: 2001* (121st edition). Washington, DC: U.S. Census Bureau.

Upchurch, Dawn M., Lee A. Lillard, and Constantijn W. A. Panis. 2001. "The Impact of Nonmarital Childbearing on Subsequent Marital Formation and

Dissolution." Pp. 344–82 in *Out of Wedlock: Causes and Consequences of Nonmarital Fertility*, edited by L. L. Wu and B. Wolfe. New York: Russell Sage Foundation.

Vaughan, Diane. 1986. *Uncoupling: Turning-Points in Intimate Relationships.* New York: Oxford University Press.

Veroff, Joseph, Elizabeth Douvan, and Richard A. Kulka. 1981. *The Inner American: A Self Portrait from 1957–1976.* New York: Basic Books.

Waite, Linda J. 1995. "Does Marriage Matter?" *Demography* 32:483–507.

Waite, Linda J. and Maggie Gallagher. 2000. *The Case for Marriage: Why Married People Are Happier, Healthier, and Better Off Financially.* New York: Doubleday.

Waite, Linda J. and Lee A. Lillard. 1991. "Children and Marital Disruption." *American Journal of Sociology* 96:930–53.

Waite, Linda J. and Glenna D. Spitze. 1981. "Young Women's Transition to Marriage." *Demography* 18:681–94.

Wallerstein, Judith S. and Sandra Blakeslee. 1989. *Second Chances: Women, Men, and Children a Decade After Divorce.* New York: Ticknor and Fields.

Wallerstein, Judith S. and Joan B. Kelly. 1980. *Surviving the Breakup: How Children and Parents Cope with Divorce.* New York: Basic Books.

Wallerstein, Judith S., Julia M. Lewis, and Sandra Blakeslee. 2002. *The Unexpected Legacy of Divorce: A 25 Year Landmark Study.* New York: Hyperion.

Webster, Pamela S., Terri L. Orbuch, and James S. House. 1995. "Effects of Childhood Family Background on Adult Marital Quality and Perceived Stability." *American Journal of Sociology* 101:404–32.

Weitzman, Lenore J. 1985. *The Divorce Revolution.* New York: The Free Press.

Wernick, Robert. 1996. "Where You Went if You Really Had To Get Unhitched." *Smithsonian*, Vol. 27, No. 3, 64–72.

White, Halbert. 1980. "A Heteroskedasticity-Consistent Covariance Matrix Estimator and a Direct Test for Heteroskedasticity." *Econometrica* 48:817–30.

White, Lynn K. and Alan Booth. 1985. "The Quality and Stability of Remarriages: The Role of Stepchildren." *American Sociological Review* 50:689–98.

Wilson, William Julius. 1987. *The Truly Disadvantaged: The Inner City, the Underclass, and Public Policy.* Chicago: The University of Chicago Press.

Winship, Christopher and Robert D. Mare. 1992. "Models for Sample Selection Bias." *Annual Review of Sociology* 18:327–50.

Winship, Christopher and Larry Radbill. 1994. "Sampling Weights and Regression Analysis." *Sociological Methodology and Research* 23:230–57.

Wojtkiewicz, Roger A. 1993. "Simplicity and Complexity in the Effects of Parental Structure on High School Graduation." *Demography* 30:701–17.

Wolfinger, Nicholas H. 1999. "Trends in the Intergenerational Transmission of Divorce." *Demography* 36:415–20.

Wolfinger, Nicholas H. 2000. "Beyond the Intergenerational Transmission of Divorce: Do People Replicate the Patterns of Marital Instability They Grew Up With?" *Journal of Family Issues* 21:1062–86.

Wolfinger, Nicholas H. 2001. "The Effects of Family Structure of Origin on Offspring Cohabitation Duration." *Sociological Inquiry* 71:293–313.

Wolfinger, Nicholas H. 2003a. "Family Structure Homogamy: The Effects of Parental Divorce on Partner Selection and Marital Stability." *Social Science Research* 32:80–97.

Wolfinger, Nicholas H. 2003b. "Parental Divorce and Offspring Marriage: Early or Late?" *Social Forces* 82:337–53.

Wolfinger, Nicholas H., Lori Kowaleski-Jones, and Ken R. Smith. 2004. "Double Impact: What Sibling Data Can Tell Us About the Negative Effects of Parental Divorce." *Social Biology* 50:58–76.

Wood, David, Neal Halfon, Debra Scarlata, Paul Newacheck, and Sharon Nissim. 1993. "Impact of Family Relocation on Children's Growth, Development, School Function, and Behavior." *Journal of the American Medical Association* 270:1334–38.

Wu, Lawrence L. 1990. "Simple Graphical Goodness-of-Fit Tests for Hazard Rate Models." Pp. 184–99 in *Event History Analysis in Life Course Research*, edited by K. U. Mayer and N. B. Tuma. Madison, WI: The University of Wisconsin Press.

Wu, Lawrence L. 1996. "Effects of Family Instability, Income, and Income Instability on the Risk of a Premarital Birth." *American Sociological Review* 61:386–406.

Wu, Lawrence L., Andrew J. Cherlin, and Larry L. Bumpass. 1987. "Family Structure, Early Sexual Behavior, and Premarital Births." Unpublished paper, Department of Sociology, University of Wisconsin-Madison.

Wu, Lawrence L. and Brian C. Martinson. 1993. "Family Structure and the Risk of a Premarital Birth." *American Sociological Review* 58:210–32.

Yamaguchi, Kazuo. 1991. *Event History Analysis*. Newbury Park, CA: Sage.

Index